GW00470015

PURBECK PARISH CHURCHES

drawn and described by **F. P. Pitfield**

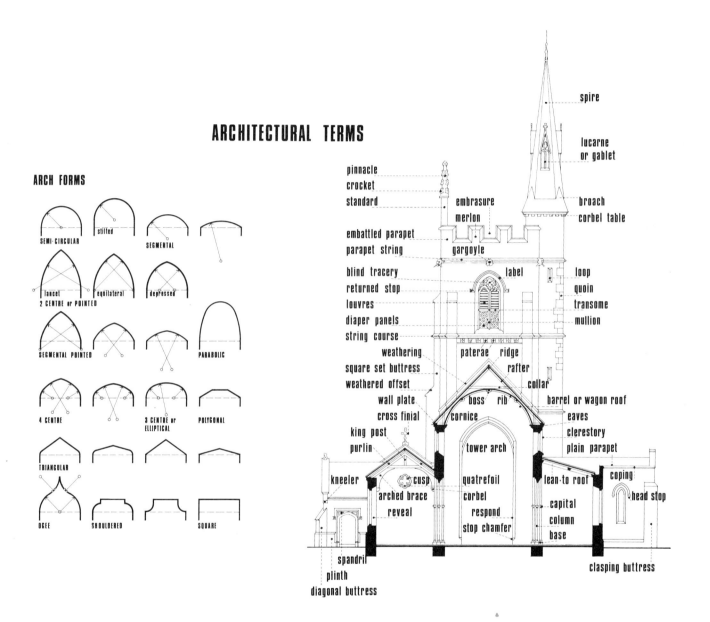

ARCHITECTURAL TERMS

ARCH FORMS

SEMI-CIRCULAR • stilted • SEGMENTAL

lancet • equilateral • depressed
2 CENTRE or POINTED

SEGMENTAL POINTED • PARABOLIC

4 CENTRE • 3 CENTRE or ELLIPTICAL • POLYGONAL

TRIANGULAR

OGEE • SHOULDERED • SQUARE

spire
lucarne or gablet
pinnacle
crocket
standard
embrasure
merlon
broach
corbel table
embattled parapet
parapet string
gargoyle
blind tracery
label
loop
returned stop
quoin
louvres
transome
diaper panels
mullion
string course
weathering
paterae ridge
square set buttress
rafter
weathered offset
collar
wall plate
boss rib
barrel or wagon roof
cross finial
cornice
eaves
king post
clerestory
purlin
tower arch
plain parapet
kneeler
lean-to roof
coping
cusp
quatrefoil
arched brace
corbel
head stop
reveal
respond
capital
stop chamfer
column
base
spandril
clasping buttress
plinth
diagonal buttress

Copyright F. P. Pitfield © 1985. All rights reserved. Typeset by Timmy Taylor at TT Typesetting with contemporary photography by Colin Graham. Printed by Andrew Johnstone and Stephen Taylor at Wincanton Litho, Old National School, North Street, Wincanton, Somerset. Casebound at Frome by Butler and Tanner Limited. Publisher: Rodney Legg. International Standard book number [ISBN] 0 902129 71 6

dpc
DORSET PUBLISHING COMPANY
KNOCK-NA-CRE, MILBORNE PORT
SHERBORNE, DORSET DT9 5HJ
First published 1985

Contents

Introduction

Any attempt to divide the county into regional areas of geological, geographical or historical significance is bound to result in anomalies where such regions adjoin each other, due to the wide geological variety found in Dorset, the way in which such natural areas tend to merge into each other, and to the changes in historical associations which have occurred over the centuries. However, the Purbeck area being in effect a peninsula bounded on the north by the shores of Poole Harbour and the River Frome, is the most clearly definable region in the county, except perhaps on the west side where its traditional limits are less clear.

A study of the origin and development of parish churches inevitably leads to a consideration of the origin of the parishes in which they occur, and although this could almost be regarded as a separate subject worthy of study in itself, it seems clear that the present day pattern of ecclesiastical parishes with which we are so familiar results from a sub-division of larger ecclesiastical territories. Before the Norman Conquest of 1066 and for some time afterwards, these larger areas were served by minster churches from which teams of priests went out to preach, or minister, in the surrounding countryside, and from the disposition of churches known to have been in existence by the time of the domesday survey of 1086, these minster areas seem likely to have been virtually the same as the judicial or administrative hundreds. The extent of the Purbeck area has thus been based upon the three domesday hundreds of Aylswood, Hasler and Winfrith together with the borough of Wareham which has always been closely associated with the Purbeck area both ecclesiastically and administratively.

Early in the 8th century three important regional churches were founded in Dorset, all at about the same time – Sherborne, which was the cathedral of Wessex until 1075 when it was transferred to Old Sarum, Wimborne, founded by Cuthberga, sister of King Ina of Wessex, and Wareham St Mary. This latter church would have been in all probability the only one in south east Dorset, serving an area well beyond the limits of Purbeck, and remaining so until the 11th century when a number of other minster churches are known to have been built. Remarkably the complete nave and aisles of this early 8th century church remained at Wareham St Mary until 1841 when regrettably they were demolished and rebuilt.

William of Malmesbury in his history of the lives of the English saints, written in about 1125, recounted a tradition that St Aldhelm, who died in 709, had founded a church in the Purbeck area near Wareham. St Aldhelm, about to set sail from Wareham, and whilst waiting for a favourable wind, returned to his family estate nearby where he is said to have built a church. The site was described as "in a district of Dorset two miles from the sea, close to Wareham, where also Corfe Castle is prominent from the sea." William of Malmesbury, writing more than 400 years after St Aldhelm's death, stated that the walls of this church were then still standing, and that although roofless, rain never fell within it, to the extent that shepherds frequently sheltered there from storms. Attempts to re-roof it by local nobles are said to have failed. During the latter part of the 19th century there were many speculations as to the whereabouts of this church of St Aldhelm's, and several parishes in the Purbeck area laid claim to it as having been the forerunner of their own church.

By the time of the domesday survey of 1086 the division of the county into 39 hundreds and four boroughs (one of which was Wareham) had become firmly established, and from the survey, read in conjunction with the earlier Geld rolls, their approximate extent can be readily determined. Their boundaries were usually natural features, particularly rivers and streams, which besides being readily identifiable, were in the case of the larger rivers, real obstacles only conveniently fordable in relatively few places. Thus the River Frome in its lower reaches quite clearly formed a firm boundary between a number of adjacent hundreds. Four churches in this area are known to have been in existence in 1086, three of them, Winfrith and two at Wareham being referred to in the survey, whilst Studland retains considerable amounts of pre-conquest work. The two churches in Wareham must have been St Martin's which still retains much pre-conquest work, and St Mary's where 8th century work survived until 1841, and significantly the distribution of the four fits well into the known pattern of the hundreds. Studland would have served Aylswood hundred, Wareham St Mary on the south side of the town would have been associated with Hasler hundred, Winfrith with Winfrith hundred, and Wareham St Martin on the north side of the town would have served an area approximating to Charborough hundred, still represented today by the large rural parish of Wareham St Martin lying to the north of the town.

During the 12th and 13th centuries a great number of new churches were built, when the former minster parishes generally became divided up into the smaller ecclesiastical parishes which still remain basically the same today. During the 12th century, whilst all four of the Purbeck minster churches were extended, rebuilt or remodelled, a priory was built at East Holme, and new churches were built at Corfe Castle, Kimmeridge,

Kingston, Steeple, Worth Matravers and probably at Coombe Keynes and Wareham Holy Trinity. This was followed in the 13th century by further churches at Arne, Church Knowle, East Stoke, Langton Matravers, Swanage, Tyneham, West Lulworth and Wool, whilst those at Coombe Keynes, Corfe Castle and Kimmeridge were enlarged. East Lulworth church was probably also first built in the 12th or 13th century as the list of known vicars goes back to 1312, but it was rebuilt in the 15th, 18th and 19th centuries and no older work survives.

By the end of the 13th century therefore the basic pattern of churches and ecclesiastical parishes had become well established, and accounts for the fact that no entirely new churches were built in the Purbeck area during the 14th and 15th centuries, nor for that matter were any of them significantly enlarged. As in Dorset as a whole, there is relatively little 14th century work. West towers were added at Church Knowle and Swanage St Mary, a north chapel was added at Wool, Wareham Holy Trinity was totally rebuilt, and the chancel at Wareham St Mary was rebuilt on an enlarged scale to remain the most impressive piece of 14th century architecture in the region.

Near the end of the 14th century, or at the beginning of the 15th a west tower was added at Corfe Castle, and later in the 15th century the roofs were renewed at a higher level. This was a fairly common practice during the 15th century when there seems to have been a demand for more spaciousness and light, to result in many churches being re-roofed and provided with larger windows. At East Lulworth a fine west tower was added, the former church at East Stoke, to judge by what remains in the ruins, was largely rebuilt, a west tower was added at Langton Matravers, and at Wareham St Martin the west end was rebuilt and new windows were inserted in the east walls of the chancel and north aisle. A west tower was added at Wareham St Mary, and at West Lulworth the old church was provided with new windows and the south tower was added or heightened. At Winfrith the nave was rebuilt and a west tower was added, whilst at Wool the nave and north aisle were rebuilt and there also a west tower was added.

Works of a similar nature continued during the first half of the 16th century when a south chapel and west tower were added at Steeple, and a north-west chapel was added at Wareham St Mary. The Reformation of the mid 16th century caused an abrupt halt in large scale structural alterations in churches, the work of the second half of the century being generally confined to relatively minor works such as the fine Clavell monument of 1572 at Church Knowle. An exception to this was at Wareham Holy Trinity where the west tower appears to have been added or rebuilt near the end of the 16th century.

Likewise during the 17th century items of the period are normally confined to internal fittings, but a north transept was added at Steeple in 1616, and later in the same century the old church of Swanage St Mary seems to have been considerably remodelled.

Considerably more work was carried out during the 18th century, particularly in internal refitting, due partly presumably to accumulated deterioration of the buildings since the Reformation, and partly to changes in taste and fashion which favoured revived classical idioms. These in their turn were viewed with an equal amount of disfavour during the latter half of the 19th century when much 18th century work disappeared mainly for that reason during the course of restorations. In 1712 the south tower of Wareham St Martin was added or rebuilt, and in 1741 the west tower at Church Knowle was to a large extent

rebuilt. Tyneham church was restored in 1744, and at nearby Creech a new church was built in 1746 partly from the ruins of Holme Priory, to be the first entirely new church built in Purbeck since the 13th century. At Studland new larger windows were installed, and the interior of Wareham St Mary was refitted. In 1774 a former south chapel at Worth Matravers was taken down, and at East Lulworth in 1787-88 the church was rebuilt on a smaller scale, retaining the 15th century west tower.

The need to provide additional accommodation in the late 18th and early 19th centuries was often overcome by the provision of galleries and although these were much disliked and removed during the latter half of the 19th century, several galleries still remain in the churches of this region. Churches of the early 19th century are characterised by a combination of continuing classical proportions and sparing amounts of Gothic detail, designed and built in accordance with the recommendations of a Parliamentary Commission resulting in rather plain and austere buildings, again much disliked and often rebuilt during the latter half of the century. Such a case is Langton Matravers where all except the tower was rebuilt in 1828, which in its turn was rebuilt again in 1875-76. East Stoke, built on a new site, also in 1828, however remains as a nearly complete example of this period, although the original small chancel was replaced by a larger one in 1885. The old church at Kingston, largely rebuilt in 1833 is another example, and the north aisle at Church Knowle with its wooden columns and gallery is also a typical addition of the 1830s. East Burton, an entirely new church of 1839-40 is of similar character, and the nave and aisles of Wareham St Mary of 1841-42, although making some concessions to the Gothic revival movement, have still, very much the air of a 'Commissioner's church'. Creech chapel, first built in 1746 but never actually brought into use as a church, was completed in 1849 in Gothic revival style following the precedent of the old Norman chancel arch re-used in the original construction.

The spate of restorations and rebuildings carried out during the second half of the 19th century may perhaps be most clearly summarised chronologically:

before 1852	Tyneham – south transept added.
1852-53	Winfrith – restored and north aisle added.
1853-54	Brownsea – new church built.
1856	Arne – minor restoration
between 1852 and 1861	Steeple – chancel rebuilt.
before 1860	Kimmeridge – partially rebuilt.
1859-60	Swanage St Mary – rebuilt except tower.
1859-60	Corfe Castle – rebuilt except tower.
1860-61	Coombe Keynes – rebuilt except tower.
1863-64	East Lulworth – rebuilt except tower.
1865-66	East Holme – new church built.
1865-66	Wool – enlarged and considerably rebuilt.
1868	Creech – chancel rebuilt.
1869-70	West Lulworth – rebuilt on new site.
1869	Worth Matravers – restoration.
1869-72	Swanage St Mark (Herston) – new church built.
1872	Kimmeridge – again partially rebuilt.
1875-76	Langton Matravers – rebuilt except tower.
1874-80	Kingston – new church built.
c 1876	Sandford new church cum school built.
1881	Studland – restoration and repairs carried out.
1882	Wareham St Mary – restoration and refit.
1885	East Stoke – chancel rebuilt.

More major works of the 20th century have included:

1903	Wareham St Mary – galleries removed and roofs of nave and aisles renewed.
1907-08	Swanage St Mary – new north aisle and transept.

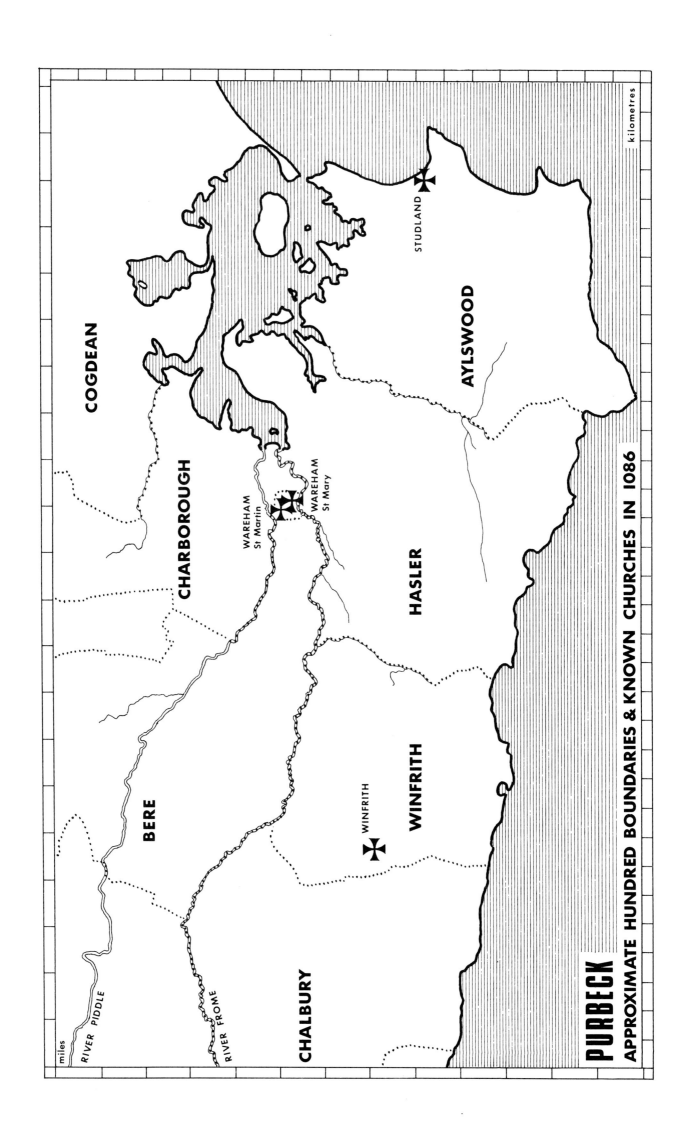

PURBECK

APPROXIMATE HUNDRED BOUNDARIES & KNOWN CHURCHES IN 1086

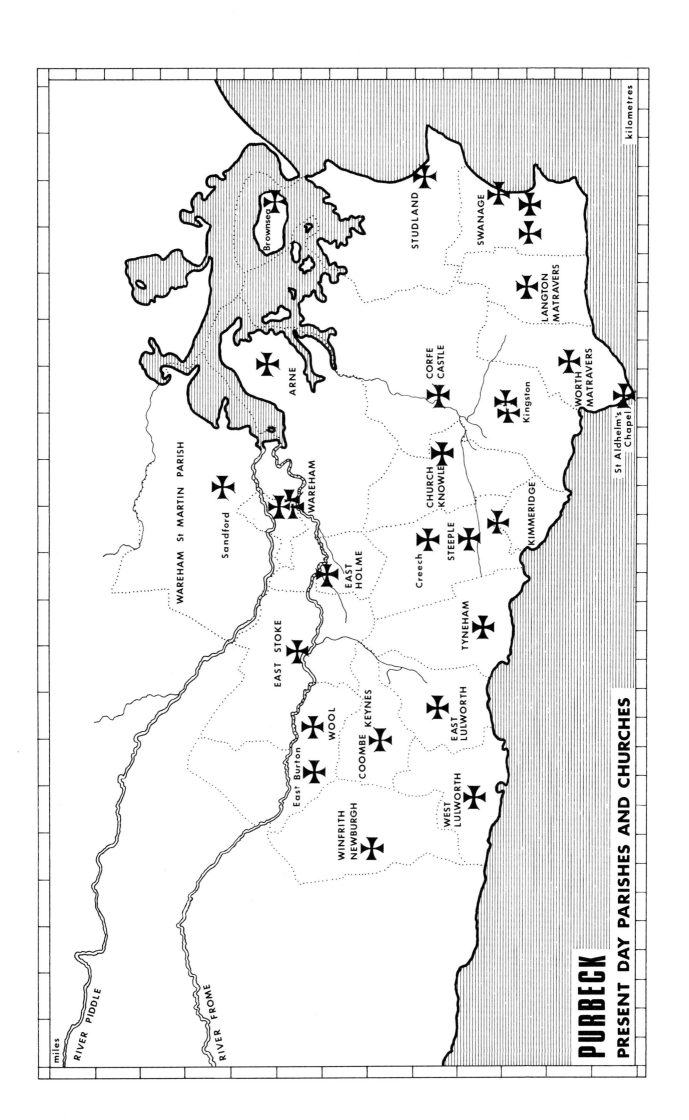

PURBECK

PRESENT DAY PARISHES AND CHURCHES

miles

RIVER PIDDLE

RIVER FROME

WAREHAM St MARTIN PARISH

Sandford

Brownsea

ARNE

WAREHAM

EAST STOKE

East Burton

WOOL

COOMBE KEYNES

WINFRITH NEWBURGH

EAST HOLME

WEST LULWORTH

EAST LULWORTH

TYNEHAM

Creech

STEEPLE

CHURCH KNOWLE

KIMMERIDGE

CORFE CASTLE

Kingston

STUDLAND

SWANAGE

LANGTON MATRAVERS

WORTH MATRAVERS

St Aldhelm's Chapel

kilometres

1908	Brownsea – south west chapel added.
1912	East Stoke – south west vestry added.
1914	Winfrith – organ chamber added.
1930	Studland – nave roof renewed.
1935-36	Wareham St Martin – restored and brought back into use.
1946-47	Corfe Castle – east end of chancel remodelled.
1956-57	Swanage All Saints – new church built.

Much has been written about the over zealous and often drastic church restorations of the 19th century. Without doubt much fine genuine mediaeval and 18th century work was needlessly destroyed, for no better reason than that it was considered "inconvenient" or "of an unsightly and unecclesiastical character". On the other hand, where old photographs have survived, it can be seen that by that time many churches were indeed in a deplorable, not to say ruinous, condition, so that such restorations, even when very drastic, can be credited at least with the saving of a building which might otherwise have disappeared altogether.

Very few churches escaped a restoration of some sort, ranging from the sympathetic version at one end of the scale, in which most of the old architectural features were retained, to complete demolition and rebuilding at the other. Almost without exception, whatever the scale of restoration, the works included internal replastering, reglazing, renewal of floors and pavings, renewal of pews and other fittings, renewal of doors, lowering of external ground levels, provision of rainwater gutters, downpipes and drains, provision of some form of heating system, reroofing and general repairs. As such works were standard practice in all restorations, they are therefore not specifically referred to in the descriptions of individual churches which follow.

Before any restoration was carried out it was necessary to deposit plans and particulars of the proposed work with the diocesan authorities in order to obtain a faculty, part of the procedure requiring the display of the faculty document on the church door for a stipulated period so that public comment and objections could be made. In effect it was a kind of ecclesiastical planning permission, except that the main concern seems to have been for the preservation and resiting of monuments and memorials and the re-allocation of seats rather than with any architectural considerations. In some cases the work was carried out without having obtained a faculty and later legalised by obtaining one in retrospect (the "parishioners having neglected to obtain a faculty") whilst in other cases the work in fact carried out was often more extensive than intended. The faculty documents formerly in the diocesan record office at Salisbury and now, since 1980, in the Wiltshire County Record Office at Trowbridge are, therefore, a valuable source of information, particularly where the submitted drawings include plans and elevations of the church as it then existed.

Other valuable sources of reference include the Dorset County Chronicle, the three editions of Hutchins' County History and Kelly's Directories. When a restored or rebuilt church was re-opened or consecrated, the Chronicle invariably carried a lengthy report on the proceedings, often in such detail that even the bishop's sermon is given verbatim. However, such accounts almost always include an historical background against which the restoration, rebuilding or provision of a new church was carried out, together with details as to what was actually done: costs, the personnel involved and donors, giving valuable supplementary information to that contained in the faculty documents.

John Hutchins' mammoth 'History and Antiquities of the County of Dorset' first appeared in two volumes in 1774, and this first edition is valuable for its descriptions of churches as they existed at that time, before any 19th century alterations had taken place, and for its descriptions of the then recent 18th century work. At the same time Hutchins' primary concern was in family histories rather than with architecture, so that, however interesting a church might have been architecturally, if it did not possess any memorials, inscriptions or heraldic devices, its basic plan form would be described and the rest dismissed with the phrase "and contains nothing remarkable". Hutchins died on 21 June 1773.

The rarer second edition, augmented into four volumes by Richard Gough, began to appear more than 20 years later – in 1796, 1803, 1813, and 1815. Although the descriptions of churches are sometimes no more than repeats from the first edition, further information is often added, particularly in the later volumes, seemingly in the form of contributed notes from the incumbents, and is consequently of more value for its church descriptions than the first edition.

The third edition, in four volumes, of 1861-70 (edited by William Shipp and James Whitworth Hodson) gives very detailed and knowledgeable architectural descriptions at a time when restorations and rebuildings were in full spate. Some of the descriptions are, therefore, of churches before restoration and some after, but in the latter case pre-restoration descriptions are sometimes given. All three editions include engravings of many churches, and those giving pre-restoration representations are of particular interest.

Kelly's directories appeared at approximately five yearly intervals and, although setting out to do no more than give a potted history of each town and village, nevertheless always included a brief description of the church and usually a date of restoration. This can sometimes be of value when a faculty might not have been obtained and a date is not otherwise known. Further very valuable information may be found in the Proceedings volumes of the Dorset Natural History and Archaeological Society (DNHAS) which have been published annually since 1877. The earlier volumes contain papers read on visits to various churches, whilst others include authoritative articles on specialised aspects of Dorset churches, most notably a first hand account of the restoration of Studland church in 1881 in volume 12, notes on church restorations in volumes 39 and 40, and the Dorset extracts of Sir Stephen Glynne's notes on English parish churches in volumes 44 and 45. Somerset and Dorset Notes and Queries (SDNQ), published regularly since 1888 also include many useful items.

The five volumes of the Royal Commission on Historical Monuments (RCHM), which now cover the whole of Dorset, based on pre-1974 boundaries, are an indispensable modern source of reference. They contain detailed descriptions of almost all old buildings built prior to 1850, those of the Purbeck area being included in Volume 2 (South-East). Pevsner's Buildings of England (Dorset) is also a useful source of reference.

A great number of parish documents are housed in the Dorset County Record Office (DCRO) and these often include correspondence, accounts, contracts and plans relating to 19th century work on parish churches, of particular interest when such work may not have been recorded at diocesan level or reported in the local press.

The Dorset County Museum collection of prints, drawings and watercolours includes many rare ones featuring churches, and these, together with the photographic collection, are of particular interest when they depict a church prior to its rebuilding, enlargement or restoration.

All these documentary sources can, therefore, be used to build up an accurate picture of a church's history during the 19th century and, to a lesser extent, for the 17th and 18th centuries. For mediaeval work, however, the building itself is generally the only source of information, and architectural evidence alone has to be relied upon for dating, apart from carved dates, initials or heraldic devices which sometimes occur, and the occasional consecration or dedication record, or will, in which the testator might have bequeathed a sum of money towards building work imminently proposed or in progress.

My indebtedness to all the above named published and documentary sources is hereby acknowledged, and I would also like to record my appreciation of the ready co-operation and assistance of the following:

The Curator and staff of the Dorset County Museum, the Dorset County Librarian and his staff, the County Archivists and their staff of the Dorset and Wiltshire Records Offices, and the Incumbents and parishioners of the churches themselves (including the custodians of keys), all those I have met during the course of my visits having been without exception most co-operative and helpful.

In the descriptions of individual churches which follow, their history and development are traced chronologically. Each illustration includes a key map of Dorset and a plan of the church, each plan being to the same scale calibrated in metres in the adjacent margins. In addition, where any church has a clearly traceable pattern of development, its probable simplified plan form at various periods is given. Detailed drawings of the more interesting old features are included within the text, and old drawings, prints or photographs of particular interest are also included.

Arne
(St. Nicholas)

THIS CHURCH is most picturesquely situated on a grassy knoll at the foot of a larger tree clad hill, and is particularly interesting in being an early 13th century building which has not been subject to any subsequent enlargements and, apart from minor alterations, remains practically as the mediaeval builders left it. The interior too still retains much of its ancient charm and simplicity, with clear glass windows giving magnificent views across the heath to Poole Harbour beyond.

The walls are almost entirely of local brown heathstone and the roofs are plain tiled with stone slate eaves courses; no doubt originally the whole of the roof was covered by stone slates.

The 13th century
Most of the structure is original 13th century work, consisting of a nave and chancel of equal width without structural division. The east window is a perfect example of a modest triple graduated lancet and, of the side windows, three on the north side and two on the south are original single lancets, although the top of the most westerly one on the north side has since been removed and replaced by a square head.

Single and triple lancet windows

There is an original 13th century doorway in the north wall of the chancel which has since been blocked, and its level indicates that the floor of the chancel was originally lower than that of the nave, following the contours of the site. This is corroborated by the fact that the sill level of the adjoining chancel lancet window is lower than the remainder.

The south doorway retains parts of the original 13th century chamfered jambs but the remainder has been rebuilt. The south porch, too, although possibly of 13th century origin, has been rebuilt with its roof at a lower level, as traces of weatherings for a higher roof remain visible on the nave wall above it. The porch arch may also be basically original work rebuilt.

The piscina in the south wall of the chancel is a plain recess with an acutely pointed head and is probably an original 13th century feature.

The piscina

The 14th century
The font is of the 14th century and consists of an octagonal bowl with two quatrefoil pointed oval recesses in each face on a plain octagonal stem and chamfered base.

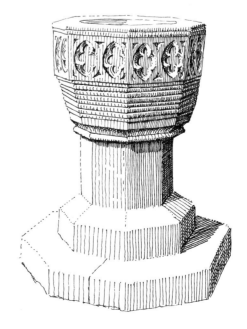
The font

ARNE
St Nicholas

Nave, south-east window

S.ᵀ NICHOLAS IN ARNE

Arne. Linen cloth of 1661 as depicted in Hutchins's 3rd edition: volume 1 (1861)

Late in the 14th century a two light window was inserted in the south wall of the nave, probably replacing a former lancet, as the remainder suggest an originally symmetrical arrangement. It was probably to provide more light for the priest, whose desk would have been in this position.

The stone altar top is of mediaeval date, and is one of the relatively few pre-reformation altar slabs to have survived in Dorset.

The 17th century

Early in the 17th century, a bell gallery was formed at the west end of the nave below roof level, together with a small unglazed opening in the west gable wall. Hutchins (1st edition: 1774) records a bell in this gallery having the initials ID:RRT and the date 1625 and, if this was the original bell, it could well mean that the gallery was erected in that year.

This could also be the year in which the roof was renewed, as some of the visible parts of the present timbers appear to be of about that date, and it would have been logical to have combined the work of re-roofing with the formation of the bell gallery. The roof is divided into five bays by collar beam trusses, although the most easterly is a tie beam truss which acts as a demarcation between nave and chancel. A plastered ceiling occurs below the level of the collars which are not visible, but the raking feet of the principals are exposed between plastered sloping soffites, and one row of purlins is exposed on each side.

The reading desk is probably of mid-19th century date, but it includes a panel carved with the initials NC and the date 1657, re-used from some earlier feature. There are two other items of 17th century woodwork – an elaborately carved oak chair and the communion rail: both having been restored and not completely original. The communion rail has round and square balusters, and the top rail is carved with an inscription based upon verse 12 of psalm 116:

I WILL RECEIVE THE CVP OF SALVATION AND CALL
VPON THE NAME OF THE LORD WITH THANKSGIVING

Hutchins' editors (3rd edition: 1861) record that a linen cloth depicting the emblems of the Trinity and dated 1661, was still at that time preserved in the church. It is said to have been the gift of William Wake, rector of Holy Trinity and St. Michael's, Wareham; the church had been a chapel of ease to Wareham Holy Trinity since the 15th century, before which time it is said to have been a chantry.

The 18th century

The church contains no 18th century work, although the present bell is said to be dated 1782. Hutchins' editors (2nd edition: 1796) say that the original bell, dated 1625, "has been lately taken down", but does not refer to a replacement.

The 19th century

The organ, which has a carved and panelled case, has the inscription "Presented by Louisa Countess of Eldon AD 1842", and still retains its brass candle holders.

Happily this church escaped the usual drastic Victorian restoration, but it was subject to a minor one in 1856, confined mainly to the renewal of seats and fittings at an estimated cost of £210. The faculty is dated 1 August 1856 and the architect was John Belcher of London. In the event, it seems that rather more work was in fact done than was disclosed on the faculty application. Hutchins' editors (3rd edition: 1861) say: "This chapel has recently undergone complete restoration at the expense of the lord of the manor," and make reference to two modern buttresses at the east end. There are five buttresses altogether and all of them seem to have been added in association with the 1856 restoration, as those on the south side appear on a drawing of 1858 by Lady Katharine Scott.

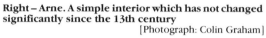

Arne. A drawing of 1858 by Lady Katharine Scott
[Source: 'Purbeck Papers'
Rodney Legg collection]

**Right – Arne. A simple interior which has not changed
significantly since the 13th century**
[Photograph: Colin Graham]

Brownsea
(St. Mary)

KING CANUTE is said to have landed on Brownsea (or Branksea) Island in 1015, and to have found there no buildings "save a chapel only", and from early times the island belonged to the monks of Cerne Abbey who were no doubt responsible for its maintenance. The chapel was still in use during the 16th century, as John Leland (1506-1552) wrote – "There is yet a chappel for an heremite. It longith to Cerne abbey", and Hutchins (1st edition:1774) stated: "The chapel was dedicated to St. Andrew, of which, and the hermitage, there are no remains."

In 1852 the island was bought by Colonel William Petrie Waugh who had been led to believe that the richest deposits of china clay in England were to be found there, but this was not the case and Colonel Waugh's clay-mining enterprises had failed by 1857 when the island again came up for sale. During his short stay, however, he spent a great deal of money on the enlargement of the castle and the building of the present church; and both these enterprises must have hastened his financial downfall, although he is said to have financed the church building "with partial assistance from Government".

The Poole and South Western Herald of 14 July 1853 carried a large engraving of the proposed church together with a report on the foundation stone laying ceremony which had taken place on 2 July "amidst at least a thousand spectators." It seems that the old chapel had not by then entirely disappeared, as Colonel Waugh had "taken particular care to preserve the small portion of the chapel wall which still remains."

Evidently the old chapel had been situated somewhere in the neighbourhood of the present church, and it is significant that the name survived into the 19th century, with the nearby shallow inlet being known as St. Andrew's Bay – until it was drained and reclaimed by Waugh in the early 1850s. This land behind the sea wall has since reverted to salt marsh.

The architect for the new church was Mr. Blanchard, the builder being Mr. Wheeler; the work was completed and consecrated on 18th October 1854 and among the distinguished guests at this function were Sir Percy and Lady Shelley. The church, as then completed, consisted of a nave, chancel with north vestry, south porch and west tower – the chapel south of the tower being a later extension. The work is in well-established Gothic-revival style, most of the windows being of 14th century type. The tower is in three stages with diagonal buttresses, embattled parapet and a stair turret on the north-east angle, the ground stage being screened across the tower arch to form a family pew.

Although the building is a good example of its time, enhanced by a beautifully landscaped setting, it is most renowned for fittings and other items of earlier date, many of which were incorporated into the original 1854 building, as they are described by Hutchins' editors (3rd edition: 1861). The most noteworthy feature is the ceiling over the family pew, in oak, divided into twelve panels by moulded beams and ribs, all richly decorated by arched braces and cusping. It is said to have come from the parlour and great chamber of Crosby Place, London built in 1446, and many 16th century panels from the same source are mounted as panelling on the walls of the family pew and chancel and incorporated into the vestry screen. The family pew is also fitted with a fireplace in the north wall, a 17th century Italian painting of the Crucifixion and an 18th century brass candelabrum.

Further treasures were later added by G. Augustus Cavendish-Bentinck, who owned the island from 1870 until 1890. They formed part of his collection of objets d'art, most from Italy and southern Europe and included, from the 16th century: a carved figure of Faith and St. Crispin, the patron saint of shoe-makers; a brass almsdish; a roundel carved with a kneeling angel; and 2 carved wooden panels depicting the Entombment and Presentation in the Temple. From the 17th century: a panelled cartouche with a shield of arms; 5 carved and gilded wooden candle-sticks decorated with acanthus foliage and angels; 2 carved panels depicting the Annunciation and Adoration of the shepherds. From the 18th century: a painted wood and plaster panel on the tower screen depicting the Annunciation; a tapestry of a landscape with birds; and brass and silver altar fittings. The grave of the Cavendish-Bentincks is in the churchyard and marked by a 16th century Italian wrought iron well-head.

A faculty application dated 13 February 1908 was for the present chapel added on the south side of the tower, to serve as a burial vault and memorial chapel for Mrs. Florence van Raalte, widow of Charles van Raalte.

BROWNSEA
St Mary

Church Knowle
(St. Peter)

HERE, AS its name suggests, is an instance of a church which has been built on a site of pre-historic significance in the form of a mound or knoll. This building is of particular interest in that it retains, in large part, its original cruciform plan together with many original features.

The 13th century

The basic walls of the nave, chancel, south transept and part of the north transept, survive from the early 13th century and contain ten original windows. Two lancets in the south wall of the nave have been almost doubled in height and a third, perhaps from the former north wall, has been reset above the porch roof. The chancel and transepts between them retain 7 two-light windows, all of which are interesting and rare examples of plate tracery,

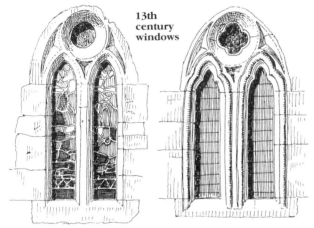

13th century windows

those of the chancel having moulded members, trefoil headed lights and cusped tracery, whilst those of the transepts are plain. The south doorways of both the nave and chancel are basically original but both have been subject to subsequent reconstruction.

The acutely pointed chancel arch is an original feature and is flanked by former altar recesses, which have since been opened up to form secondary openings into the chancel. The arch to the south transept was rebuilt to a greater height in the 19th century but much of the original 13th century material seems to have been re-used. The north wall of the nave was removed in adding the 19th century north aisle but a 13th century doorway, now under the gallery stairs, could have been the former north door, whilst the top of the south squint appears to be formed in part from a piece of old window head.

A Purbeck stone altar top with five original consecration crosses, now set up in the south transept, may be an original feature and was discovered in 1927 doing duty as a floor slab in the north aisle. Other 13th century items include a piscina in the south transept, complete with its original bowl, another in the chancel, with a later 16th century bowl, and parts of two coffin lids.

Piscinae

The 14th century

The west tower was added early in the 14th century and, although largely rebuilt in 1741, the lower parts of the walls, the tower arch and two small rectangular windows are original. The south porch is an addition to the original building and perhaps also of 14th century date. There is a stoup in the north east angle of the porch internally, moved to that position in 1956 after having been built into the west wall, presumably in order to avoid its destruction at the time of the Reformation.

Stoup in porch

Interior, showing the 13th century chancel arch and flanking openings, and the 19th century wooden north arcade columns and north gallery
[Photograph: Colin Graham]

CHURCH KNOWLE
St Peter

CHURCH KNOWLE development

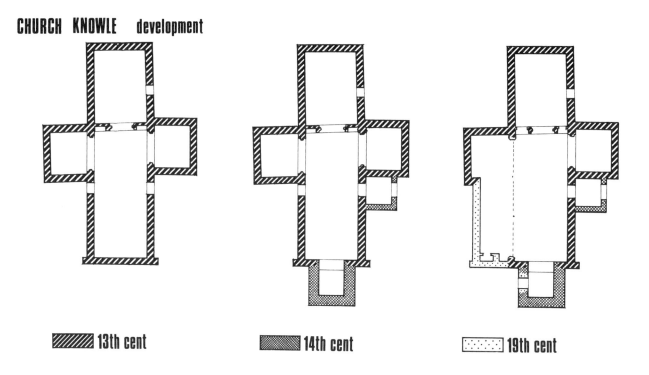

▨▨▨ 13th cent   ▨▨▨ 14th cent   ⬚⬚⬚ 19th cent

The 15th century

Work during this century was confined to the insertion of a three-light square headed window in the south wall of the chancel, no doubt replacing an earlier one, and the formation of plain squints from the transepts to the chancel, that on the north side projecting externally and supported on corbelling.

Chancel south-east window

Clavell monument

The 16th century

Apart from the bowl of the chancel piscina, the most noteworthy survival from this period is the splendid Clavell monument in the form of a richly carved canopied altar tomb against the east wall of the north transept, which entailed blocking the 13th century window behind it. It is complete with brasses, dated 1572, and typical of such monuments of the period, being very similar to the Skerne monument of 1596 at Bere Regis.

A band of floral and foliage mural painting around the perimeters of the chancel arch and its flanking arches on the nave side may be of 16th century origin, but it has been extensively repainted.

The 17th century

Work of this century is represented in parts of the communion table, a table at the west end and two carved chairs in the chancel. Another small oak table in the chancel is of late 17th or early 18th century date.

The 18th century

Except for the lower part, the tower was rebuilt in 1741, as a stone tablet on the south wall externally bears that date and the initials of the churchwardens, IC and EC. It is plain, without buttresses or string courses, has small rectangular louvred belfry windows in the north, west and south faces and a distinctive stone-slated pyramid roof.

The 19th century

During the incumbency of the Rev. J. L. Jackson (1833-41), the north aisle was added and involved the removal of much of the north transept and its roof, thereby destroying the characteristic cruciform plan arrangement which had, until that time, survived. The work is typical of the 1830s and included the replacement of the north wall of the nave by a beam, supported on two slender square wooden columns which play a dual role in supporting the contemporary gallery which extends throughout the north aisle and across the west end of the nave. Unusually all the work of this period, including the gallery, remains and was not replaced later in the century as was so often the case.

The original north gable of the transept was removed and the whole incorporated under a continuous double pitched roof. The north windows are plain pairs of lancet lights, with a single lancet in the upper part of the east gable and a two-light window in the west gable similar to those in the chancel. At the same time the nave roof was renewed at a higher level, with a plastered ceiling divided into three bays by traceried tie beam trusses with arched collar braces which produce a pseudo hammer beam effect. In conjunction with this general heightening, the original lancets in the south wall of the nave were elongated to their present extent. The south transept seems also to have been heightened, as the arch to the nave was rebuilt to a greater height.

The hexagonal oak pulpit is of a similar date and probably formed part of the work of this period, but the organ was built by J. W. Walker of London in 1858 and it seems to have been necessary to adapt the west gallery in order to accommodate it, as the organist's seat is cantilevered out so that its back and sides form a central raised and projecting portion.

Oak panelling with a central cross and side standards, now against the west wall of the south transept, appears to have been a former reredos since removed, perhaps in 1891 as, according to Kelly's directory, the chancel was restored in that year. The timber roof of the chancel would, therefore, be of that date.

Coombe Keynes
(Holy Rood)

ALTHOUGH LARGELY rebuilt in 1860-61 this church is noteworthy for its original 13th century tower which has a distinctive Purbeck stone slated pyramidal roof. Doubtless this roof has been renewed several times since the 13th century but the original form is likely to have been retained, as there is reason to believe that many early towers might have been roofed in this way. It is perhaps significant that this traditional form of tower roof should have survived at several places in the Purbeck area, where stone slates continued to be available for repairs and renewals.

The 13th century

The original building seems to have survived complete until the 19th century, according to the description of Hutchins (1st edition:1774): "The church of Comb-Keins stands at the south end of the parish. It is an ancient, low, and dark fabric. There are several very long and narrow lancet windows in the chancel and the west end of the tower. It consists of a chancel, body, and south isle, equal to the body, and divided from it by three arches. The tower is low and tiled, and in it are three bells. In the chancel, on the south side against the wall, are two low altar tombs, very ancient, especially the westernmost, but no marks of any inscription."

The south aisle referred to was evidently of 13th century origin, as the westernmost of the three arcade arches was re-used to form the present chancel arch which is of that date. The population of the village must therefore have declined between the 13th and 19th centuries, as the rebuilding of 1860-61 omitted the south aisle, to result, unusually, in a reduction in size. Hutchins' editors (3rd edition:1861) and the Dorset County Chronicle of 29 August 1861 refer to the re-use of older features including "several of the original windows," but,

apart from the chancel arch, only one other feature – one of the lancet windows in the north wall of the chancel – appears to be of 13th century origin.

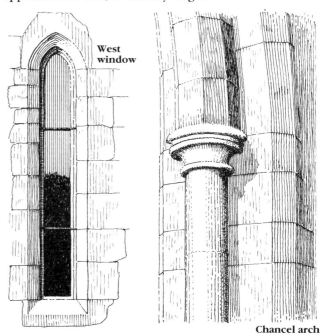

West window

Chancel arch

The basic wall structure of the tower is original and includes a contemporary long lancet west window, and above it a stone louvred lancet belfry window. There is no tower arch as such to the nave, but there is instead a 13th century doorway with a lancet opening in the wall above it, possibly the original arrangement, but more probably an 1860-61 adaptation in which a former external doorway and window were re-used. The hemispherical font bowl is also an original 13th century feature but it is now in Wool Church.

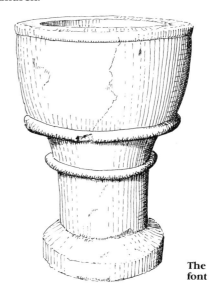

The font

The 14th – 17th centuries

The three bells, which are now in the Dorset County Museum at Dorchester, are of interest, particularly the first bell which was cast by Thomas Hey in the mid 14th century and inscribed "Angelus. Michael. Maria. Gabriel." The second bell is inscribed "Anthony Bond made me. 1636", and the third "Love God. I. W. 1599", the initials being those of John Wallis a well-known Salisbury bell-founder.

No account of Coombe Keynes church would be complete without reference to the famous silver chalice which dates from about the year 1500, being one of only

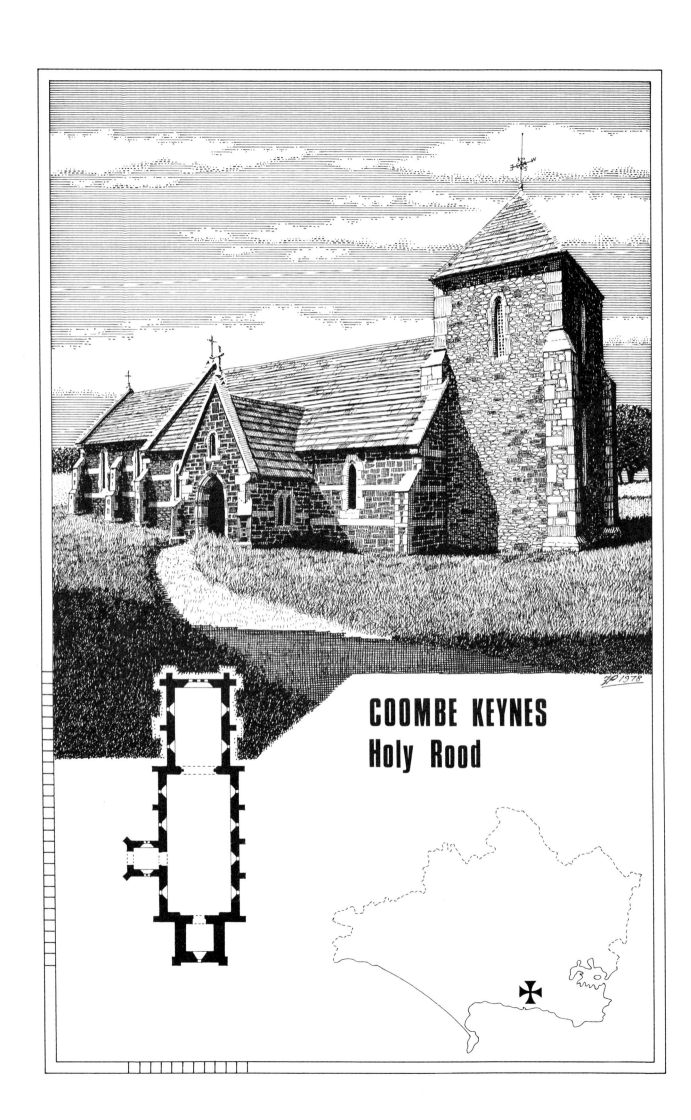

COOMBE KEYNES
Holy Rood

three pieces of pre-Reformation plate to have survived in Dorset. It is a beautiful and well preserved specimen, and has been on permanent loan to the Victoria and Albert Museum since 1930. The cup is rounded, on a hexagonal stem with a projection or 'knot' in the form of six spirally twisted lobes ending in crowned angel's heads, and the base is flared to a concave sided hexagon with six knops at the points in the form of floriated initials 'M'. One panel of the flared base is engraved with a representation of the crucifixion.

The chalice.
Illustration
from Nightingale's
'Church Plate
of Dorset'

The 19th century

In the 13th century the village must have been considerably larger than it is now, for the church then had a south aisle and was the parochial church of both Coombe Keynes and Wool, the latter church having only the status of a chapel under its jurisdiction. Possibly the Black Death of 1348 may have been primarily responsible for the decline in population, as a generation later the parishioners of Wool petitioned for a greater measure of independence, as recorded by Hutchins (1st edition: 1774):-

"In 1380 a composition was made between the inhabitants of the parish of Comb-Keines, the chapel of Wool, and the rectory of the prior of Merton. The chapel had all parochial rights, ab antique, except sepulture. And the inhabitants, who used to bury at Comb-Keins, desire that the chapel and cemetery may be consecrated for the burial of the dead. The parishioners of Wool were to repair their chapel. This composition was not then fully carried into execution; but, upon an allegation of the disagreement of the inhabitants of both vills about the fabric of the body of the chapel, the inclosure of the churchyard, and the ornaments of the church, it was decreed, 30 March, 1384, that the chapel and cemetery should be dedicated" ...

So, after 1384 Wool enjoyed most of the privileges of a parish church, but it nevertheless remained a chapel to Coombe Keynes until becoming a separate parish in 1844.

By the middle of the 19th century the south aisle had evidently been disused for many years according to the notes of Sir Stephen Glynne who visited the church on 19 June 1849:-

"A small church comprising a nave with south aisle, chancel, western tower, and north porch. The arcade between the nave and aisle has three pointed arches, with continued mouldings down square piers which have no

capitals, excepting the western arch which rises from a shaft set against the pier. The chancel arch is low and semi-circular on imposts. In the aisle (which has a separate tiled roof) are two lancets on the south – the south-western of which is a lychnoscope – and there are two on the north. The east window is square-headed of three lights and late. Some other bad windows have been introduced. The walls are of flint and stone. The south aisle damp from the accumulation of earth and disused. The font a circular cup upon a cylinder. The tower low, without buttresses, having a pointed roof: on its west side a long lancet and lancet belfry window. The roofs are chiefly of stone flags."

From this account it would appear that although most of the features described were of 13th century date, the semi-circular chancel arch was a Norman one, suggesting that an original 12th century church had been rebuilt and enlarged in the 13th century incorporating at least one of the older portions.

In a report dated 7 August 1858, T. H. Wyatt, the diocesan architect and surveyor described the extremely dilapidated state of the building:-

"I have never seen a sadder case than this of Ecclesiastical dilapidation and difficulty, a portion of the Church is a complete ruin and the rest little better. ... The South Aisle is the part in ruins, and what remains must be taken down ... and I shall advise that the arcade between the Nave and Aisle be taken down, and the south wall built on the old foundations, using in again the old stone in walls and windows. The Piers and arches already overhang considerably, and are hardly safe. The north wall of the Nave is very bad, leaning outwards considerably, particularly above the arching the window sills. It is indispensable to take this down. ... There are some serious settlements and cracks in the lower part of the Tower, but these, I think are capable of being made sound with judicious underpinning, bonding in and general repairs. The upper part of the Tower is however in a very dangerous condition; the wall bulging considerably: the roof nearly off: and the wet pouring down in streams: the Bell framing rotten and dangerous, and about half the south wall split and forced out by a great ivy root or tree. At least 10 or 12 ft. of the upper part and half the south wall of the Tower must be rebuilt."

After such an alarming report a major restoration was inevitable, and a faculty for rebuilding is dated 22 June 1860. The architect was John Hicks of Dorchester (for whom Thomas Hardy worked as a pupil and assistant 1856-62), and the estimated cost was £662. The work included complete rebuilding to a smaller size, omitting the former south aisle, but retaining the old tower which was repaired and strengthened. Clasping buttresses were added to the western angles and additional lancet belfry windows were added in the north and south walls.

The work of 1860-61 is in 'Early English' style in repetition of the old work, the walls being generally of brown heathstone with ashlar bonding courses and dressings, the roofs stone slated and the windows of single lancet form, except the east window which is a graduated triplet. The roofs internally are plastered between exposed rafters and divided into bays by arch braced principals. The two old altar tombs referred to by Hutchins are said to have been "placed on the ground to the north and west of the porch." The actual cost of the work was surprisingly close to, in fact slightly below, the estimated cost stated in the faculty. The builder John Wellspring of Dorchester, was paid £595. 2s. 6d., whilst John Hicks' fee was £45, making £640. 2s. 6d. in all, but other incidental expenses including £36. 9s. 0d. spent on the consecration day celebrations brought the amount to over £700.

The Dorset County Chronicle of 29 August 1861 included a full report on the consecration service and celebrations, together with a graphic account of the state of the old church:-

"Time had made sad inroads upon the old building, which was in the Early English style of architecture, consisting of a quaint old tower, nave, south aisle and chancel. The ivy had crept through numerous crevices in the walls, and flourished luxuriantly inside the sacred edifice, nor was there any lack of moisture and fresh air from the dilapidated condition of the roof. In short, the place was in a wretched condition, the south aisle having neither floor nor pews, while here were the bells which ought to have been in the tower, with the debris of the stocks and wheels with which they had formerly been hung. Combe Keynes is the mother church of Wool, and as suggested by the size of the original building, there was no doubt years ago a much larger population here than is now the case, for in a field adjoining the churchyard there are the remains of the foundations of a number of houses."

"The melancholy state of the church had long been a subject of anxiety to the clergy who have successively held the living, and a considerable time since Mr. Hicks, architect, of Dorchester, had been called in to report on the subject... Owing to the peculiar circumstances in which the parish was situated, liberal subscriptions were given by the surrounding clergy and gentry, grants were obtained from the diocesan and incorporated societies, and a praiseworthy feature is the readiness with which the inhabitants came forward and voted a rate of £100. By these means the church has now been re-built, with the exception of the tower, in strict keeping with the original building, as much of the old work being preserved as possible, and several of the Early English windows are re-inserted, though, of course, the architect has avoided the inconsistent, square-headed, perpendicular windows which had been put in years ago, when some portions of the edifice had been repaired. Thus the parish of Combe Keynes has now a structure which is a very pretty object in the surrounding wooded landscape, and while simplicity pervades the internal arrangements, the general effect is pleasing in the extreme... The westernmost arch of the arcade which formerly separated the nave by three bays from the south aisle, has been cleaned and restored, and now pleasingly divides the nave from the chancel of the new building, while a chaste triplet window has been inserted in the west (sic) wall of the chancel, filled with lily pattern quarries, by Bell, of Bristol, the sacred monogram being displayed in the centre. We may here also mention that the two pretty little windows on each side of the chancel are also filled with painted glass on the diaphene principle, tastefully executed by the vicar, and having figures on a blue ground with a neat border, representing the four Evangelists, together with St. Peter, St. Paul, and John the Baptist... In order to render the place free from damp, and to improve its general appearance, the floor has been raised and the ground cleared away on the south side... As previously hinted, the tower has only been restored, buttresses having been run some distance up the two outer angles, and the work generally repaired, the three sweet little bells having been re-hung. The restoration was executed after the plans of Mr Hicks, who was highly complimented for the taste he had displayed, and the work has been admirably carried out by Mr. Wellspring, builder, of Dorchester.

"On Saturday morning last, the bells, which had so long been silent, once again sent forth their joyous summonses, the Lord Bishop of Salisbury having appointed that day for the consecration of the new edifice."

The 20th century

During this century a further decline in the population of the village led to the church being declared redundant on 14 January 1974, and various attempts since then to devise a suitable use for the building in order to ensure its preservation culminated in the formation of the Combe Keynes Trust in 1980. In 1981 the church was conveyed to the Trust which has commendably raised funds and begun a programme of repairs, not only to preserve the building, but so that it can be used for educational, recreational and leisure purposes for the benefit of the community.

Corfe Castle
(St. Edward the Martyr)

HERE THE village and its church are overshadowed, not only figuratively but literally, by its renowned castle, and the fate of both must have been closely tied over the centuries to developments and events concerning the castle itself. Although the castle originated in the 11th century, or possibly even earlier, its principal development occurred during the 12th and 13th centuries, and the growth of the village and church can be expected to have followed a similar pattern. This is confirmed by the existence of 12th and 13th century remains in the present church and, although its development cannot be traced with any certainty, due to almost total rebuilding in 1859-60, 18th and early 19th century descriptions, together with the faculty plan of 1859 give a good guide as to the building's probable development.

Hutchins (1st edition: 1774) described the old church as it then was:

"It is dedicated to St Edward the Martyr, and is a large and ancient fabric, in which are several narrow, long lancet windows. It consists of a nave covered with lead, a chancel, and two isles tiled. The isles are higher than the body, but of equal length with the chancel and nave, as far as the church porch, which is very large. Between that and the tower, are on each side additional buildings, which might have been chapels. That on the S. side is now a vestry, and consistory court; that on the N. a lumber room. The tower is very large, embattled, and pinnacled: in it are five bells a clock, and chimes. On the sides of the belfry door are two empty niches. Under that, on the right, is a group of three human busts, with something twisted round their necks. In the middle of the group is a small human figure, which has the head of a hog. Under that, on the left side, are two such figures. The body is supported by twelve unequal arches. The four pillars on the porch are of the Saxon style, but each different. The rebels battered the castle from the church, which received damage from thence; for, in 1646, the committee paid £50 to repair it."

Sir Stephen Glynne visited the church on 7 October 1825, and his more architecturally knowledgeable account supplements that of Hutchins:

"The town is poor and of forlorn appearance. The church is a good structure, in very good repair, and

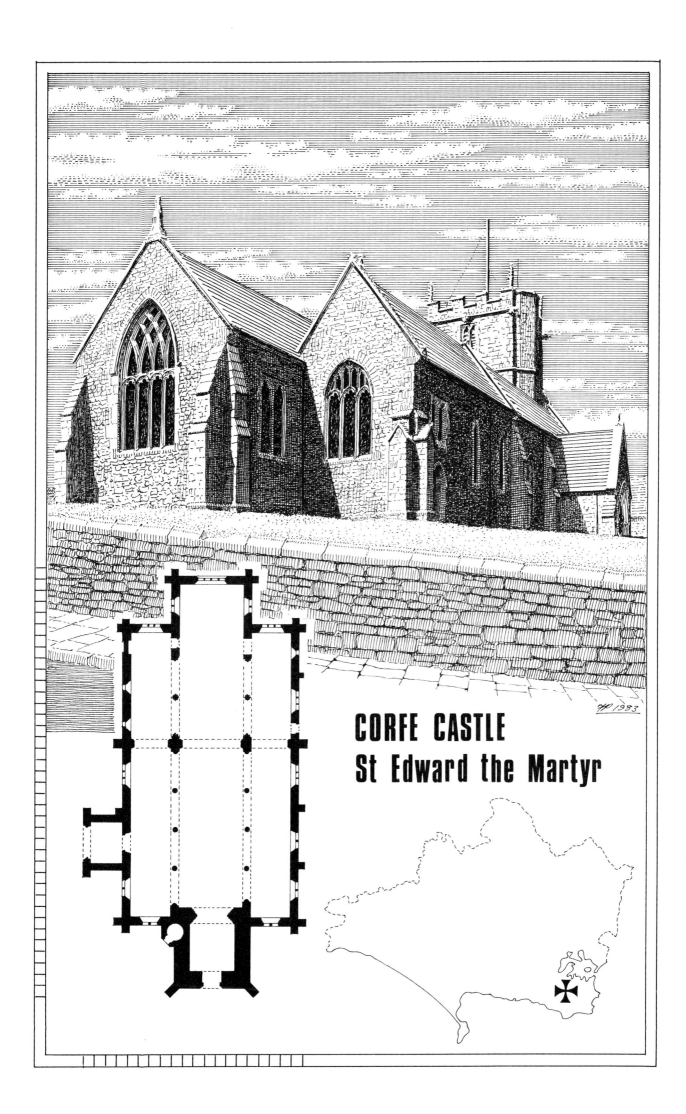

CORFE CASTLE
St Edward the Martyr

CORFE CASTLE   probable development

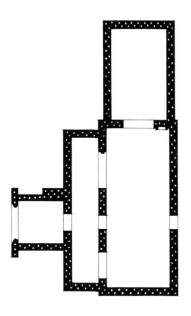

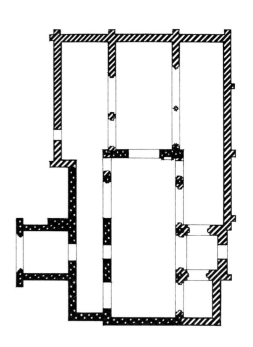

██████ 12th cent

▨▨▨▨ 13th cent

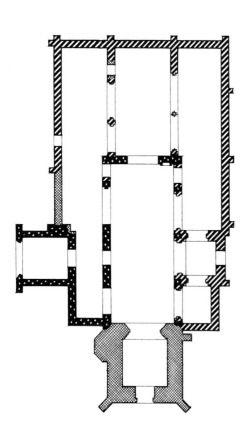

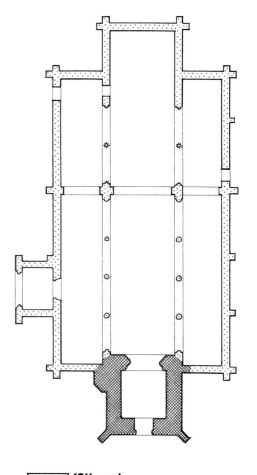

▓▓▓▓ 14th cent

▒▒▒▒ 19th cent

consisting of a nave with side aisles, a chancel, and a tower at the west end containing six bells. The tower is perpendicular, and has four pinnacles and an octagonal staircase turret, and opens to the Church by a pointed arch. The nave is divided from the aisles by pointed arches, of which the eastern ones are very narrow and small. The piers are plain, having Early English brackets. The clerestory has small square-headed Perpendicular windows. The greater part of the windows have good Decorated tracery. The chancel has some lancet windows; but the eastern one is a very fine Decorated one of rather an early period, with three lights, having arches and trefoils. The chancel is divided from the south side by two very fine pointed arches with very deep architrave mouldings, springing from a round pier surrounded by clustered slender shafts of Purbeck marble. On the north side the pier is plain and unornamented. The arch from the nave to the chancel is semi-circular. The font is octagonal, upon an octagonal pedestal with good Perpendicular pannelling and quatrefoils."

These two descriptions, read in conjunction with the faculty plan of 1859 which shows the building as it existed before rebuilding, enable the probable development of the church to be deduced.

The 12th century

By the 12th century the church must have been a large structure, consisting of a nave and chancel the same size as their present counterparts (except that the chancel stopped some 4.3m. short of the present east end and was slightly narrower) a narrow north aisle and a large north porch. This latter feature is shown on the faculty plan to be retained, and Hutchins' editors (3rd edition: 1861) say: "This fine relic of the ancient edifice has been restored, and the work of the outer arch rechiselled all over." Although the work appears to be 19th century imitation rather than restoration, the present porch is in its original position and of exactly the same plan form as before, although adapted internally to suit the widening of the aisle at that point. From the faculty plan, the nave arcades were not true arcades as such, but rather walling pierced by individual arches of varying widths particularly on the north side where the western half of the aisle itself was much narrower and where probably parts at least of the original 12th century arcade may have survived – perhaps a 12th century capital with a chevron ornamented abacus and foliage carving, now lying loose in the church, may have formed part of one of the north arcade arches. The end of the north aisle west of the porch had at some time been partitioned off with a separate entrance from outside, and this part, referred to by Hutchins as a lumber room, is labelled 'Bone House' on the 1859 faculty plan.

The 13th century

During this period the church seems to have been enlarged by the addition of a south aisle to the nave, and aisles to both sides of the chancel, bringing the building to almost its present size. This work may have been carried out at two distinctly different times, coinciding approximately with the early and later 13th century enlargements of the castle. From the faculty plan the south arcade of the nave – of three equal arches plus a narrower doorway-like opening at the east end – was supported on simple sections of walling with responds of two chamfered orders; and the north arcade of the chancel, of two arches, was similar. However, the two arches of the chancel south arcade were more elaborate

and probably of later date, the central pier and responds being of clustered shafts.

Much of the material still remains in the arches on both sides of the chancel, in the form of arch voussoirs of two bead moulded orders, and the fact that the clustered shaft column and responds on the south side were shown as existing work to be retained may indicate that they are basically of 13th century origin. Hutchins (1st edition: 1774) mentions "several, long, lancet windows" and four of these, two in each side wall of the chancel aisles, are shown on the faculty plan. One of them has been re-used internally above the doorway between the chancel and its north aisle. The former east window described by Sir Stephen Glynne as a fine example of early Decorated work is also likely to have been of late 13th century date, suggesting that the east end of the chancel might have been rebuilt or remodelled in conjunction with the addition of the chancel aisle on the south side. According to the faculty plan the centre bay of the south aisle was structurally divided from the remaining bays and the nave by archways, and with an external door in the south wall forming a porch-like feature. The walls forming this compartment were about 1 metre thick suggesting that it might have been originally a 13th century south tower, the upper part of which had been taken down and the remainder incorporated into the south aisle when the present tower was later added.

Other remains of this period, re-used in 1859-60 from former positions, include a narrow archway in the south wall of the chancel (now containing the organ console), a foliage carved capital now forming part of the most easterly pier of the nave south arcade, and a carved piscina bowl reset in a modern rectangular recess in the chancel north aisle.

Reused lancet window

13th century arch springing

13th century capital

Piscina

The 14th century

Due to the considerable enlargements carried out during the 13th century, the church seems not to have been significantly altered during this period, although many of the earlier windows must have been replaced as Sir Stephen Glynne says: "The greater part of the windows have good Decorated tracery." Surviving 14th century features include the doorway between the chancel and its north aisle, and a stone corbel carved with oak leaves and acorns.

Near the end of the 14th century or beginning of the 15th the present west tower was added. It is of three stages with an embattled and pinnacled parapet and large gargoyles at the angles and mid points. There are diagonal buttresses at the west angles and an octagonal stair turret, entered externally since 1860 but formerly from inside.

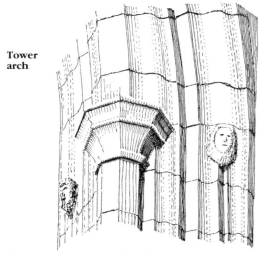

Tower arch

The tower arch is high, of two wave moulded orders, the outer continuous and the inner springing from semi-octagonal jamb shafts and with carved heads of a man on one side and a woman on the other. The west doorway has a high triangular arch with traceried spandrils containing shields, one set sideways, and large label stops in the form of male and female busts. Flanking it are canopied niches for images now gone, on carved corbels, one of which depicts a man, playing bagpipes, and a monkey. Above, the west window is of three lights with unusual intersecting tracery, and the belfry windows are each of two trefoil headed lights in square heads.

The blank shields in the spandrels of the west doorway would originally have been painted as shields of arms, and A. W. Vivian-Neal, writing in Somerset and Dorset Notes and Queries (Vol. 27, p 158-159) put forward an interesting and convincing theory to account for one of them being set sideways, and for the pairs of male and female head carvings which appear on the tower arch and west doorway. Such carvings are thought to usually

West window

West doorway

represent donors of work, and he observed that the unusually large busts which form the label terminations of the west doorway were dressed in costume of c. 1400, and suggested that they might represent John Beaufort and his wife. Beaufort, who was legitimated on 9 February 1397, was married shortly afterwards and succeeded his father-in-law as Constable of Corfe Castle the same year, holding the office until his death in 1409. As his arms were changed upon legitimation, his former arms may have been painted on the shield which is set sideways.

The 15th century

The font is of Purbeck marble having an octagonal bowl carved with quatrefoiled panels, supported by an octagonal stem with cinquefoil headed panels. Of similar date is a pair of finely worked, and elaborate, Purbeck marble standards now standing loose on either side of the tower arch, which may have originally formed part of a reredos.

The former clerestory windows are said to have been of Perpendicular type, suggesting that the nave roof was renewed during the 15th century at a higher level, and the chancel roof was probably renewed at about the same time as ten late 15th or early 16th century roof bosses from it were salvaged in 1859 and mounted on the present chancel wall plates. One represents a crown and the remainder have foliage carving, four including individual Lombardic letters O, H, W and C. One is inscribed on the back – "CC OLD CHURCH MAY 1859 from THE CHANCEL ROOF" with the initials of the rector, curates and churchwardens.

The
font

The 17th century

During the civil wars the church suffered heavily as a result of the long siege of the castle, when the church was used by the Parliamentary forces as a vantage point. – "The most advantageous point of their batteries was the Church, which they, without fear of profanation, used, not only as their rampart but their rendezvous. Of the surplesse they made two shirts for two soldiers, they broke down the organs and made the pipes serve for cases to hold their powder and shot, and, not being furnished with musket-bullets, they cut off the lead of the church, and rolled it up and shoot it without even casting it in a mould." In addition horses are said to have been stabled in the church, using the font as a drinking trough, and a cannon is said to have been mounted on the roof of the tower. As recorded by Hutchins the Parliamentary Committee made a grant of £50 in 1646 towards the cost of repairing the damage.

Survivals from this period include the royal arms of Charles II dated 1660, and a small chest made by Henry Paulet in 1672 at a cost of 8s. 0d.

Chest
of 1672

For some peculiar reason, the separate room at the west end of the south aisle, which could only be entered from inside the church, had for many years been used for the storage of lime, but the inconvenience which this must have caused was resolved in 1698 when it was converted into a vestry.

The 19th century

The 19th century restoration was of the most drastic kind, in which much more work was carried out than originally proposed. The faculty is dated 21 April 1859, the architect was T. H. Wyatt and the estimated cost of £2350 was for taking down and rebuilding "nearly the whole of the external Walls except those of the Porch and Tower," re-roofing the nave, north aisle and the western

end of the south aisle, the removal of an "unsightly Mausoleum" in the south east angle of the chancel south aisle, removal of the galleries and renewal of all internal fittings. It had been intended to retain much of the interior arcading, the roofs of the south aisle and chancel, together with the east wall of the chancel, but in the event all except the tower was almost, if not totally, rebuilt and the chancel lengthened eastwards. At the same time the width of the chancel was increased to equal that of the nave.

Some old features already referred to were incorporated, but most of the work was entirely new in imitation of former, mostly 13th century, features. Of the new windows, some are in the form of lancets whilst others are of plate or vertical traceried types. The nave arcades are of circular columns and arches of 13th century type and the aisles are separated from those of the chancel by arches in the same plane as the chancel arch, all expressed externally by buttresses and roof parapets.

The chancel roof is of exposed boarding and rafters, divided into four bays by arch-braced collar principals. The nave roof is of plaster between exposed rafters, divided into four bays by arch and cross braced principals springing from wall posts off foliage carved wall corbels. The roofs of all the aisles are of trussed rafter construction. The alabaster and marble reredos, designed by G. E. Street, was added in 1876.

The preparations for rebuilding were reported in two issues of the Dorset County Chronicle, the first being of 24 February 1859:

"We are pleased to hear that it is decided to restore this ancient edifice, which perhaps is coeval with the old castle. The building has, we believe, been pronounced unsafe for public worship for a much longer period, the out-walls projecting nearly one foot beyond the perpendicular. A list of subscriptions already promised towards this desirable object was read at a late vestry meeting, and there is no doubt but liberal donations will continue to come in from the many resident gentry in the island as the work progresses."

Commencement of the work was reported in the issue of 12 May 1859:

"The contract for the restoration of our church is taken by Farwell and Meadus, the former a builder of Swanage, the latter of Poole. The work was commenced on Wednesday last. The services will be conducted at present in the National Schoolroom, and for the accommodation of our people there will be a cottage lecture in some part of the parish once or twice a week, besides one, and sometimes two, services at Bushay Chapel each Sabbath, and two more at the chapel of Kingston. What is lost, therefore, by the larger assembly at church, will be more than counterbalanced by the number of services performed at the different places indicated."

The completed church was consecrated on 23 July 1860, and reported in the Dorset County Chronicle of 26 July:

"The above church, which, with the exception of the tower, has been entirely rebuilt and enlarged, was re-opened and consecrated by the Lord Bishop of the Diocese, on Monday last. The attendance of the clergy was somewhat extensive, but the general attendance, which there is no doubt would have been very great had the weather been more propitious, was sadly limited – a down-pour of rain setting in early in the morning, and continuing without intermission throughout the day. Every preparation had been made, not only by those in authority, but by the inhabitants in general. All the shops were kept strictly closed, and the proceedings of the day, in connection with the completion of the sacred edifice, were looked forward to by all classes as of singular interest. At early dawn a peal from the bells in the old tower was the signal note for all; flags and banners were unfolding, waving from many of the private residences, especially in the neighbourhood of the church, the tower of the latter being surmounted by one of extra size. Immediately before the gates near the Cross, two floral emblems, designed with considerable taste, were erected, and the path leading from the steps to the entrance of the church was completely enclosed and covered in with large branches of laurels, &c. On entering the church the appearance and general arrangement of the fabric was imposing and effective. The old church, which for centuries had occupied the site of the present erection, was a blending of various styles of architecture in a somewhat confused mass, the predominating one being early English; and to this latter style the architect, Mr T. H. Wyatt, has with much tact principally adhered in the restoration... The roof of the chancel is an open one of stained wood. The corbels supporting the vaulting shafts are very tastefully carved; but we sought in vain the corbels of the original chancel, which, if our recollection bear us out, were much more characteristic of the period than the leaves and flowers that have replaced them. ... In the north porch the two original Saxon shafts have been restored and built in with the new work. ... Mr T. Farwell, of Swanage, and Mr Meadus, of Poole, were the builders, and their work has been exceedingly well executed.

"The festivities, which were postponed on Monday, in consequence of the rain, took place on the following day with great eclat, the whole population of the place being invited to take part in the joyous event without distinction. Upwards of 600 children from the different schools were entertained to tea with plenty of plum cake, in the grounds of the interesting old castle; the old women were supplied with ¼lb. of tea, and the labourers in the parish were presented with 3lbs. of beef each, so that all had ample means of enjoying themselves."

Evidently the reporter, presumably due to the inclement weather, did not research the project to the Chronicle's usual degree of thoroughness, for the following week's issue, of 2 August 1860, included a supplementary report aimed at correcting some errors and omissions:

"In the hasty sketch of our correspondent, on the opening of the above church on Monday, the improvements that have been made in the removal of several old cottges that completely surrounded and hid the old church were omitted. This has taken place at the eastern end of the church, by which a good view of the sacred edifice is now obtained, and it is hoped and contemplated that ultimately most of the other erections will be done away with, when the beauty of the restoration will be so much more apparent. Although the weather on the day of the opening prevented many individuals from remaining till the evening service, yet, happily for the near residents, the rain ceased about six o'clock, and a full attendance was the consequence – every part of the church was crowded.

"By an error in transcribing from very scattered remarks, some portions of our descriptions we have since discovered to be incorrect. Among them the east window should have been described as having very elegant tracery in-the decorated style of architecture; and that arches in the nave are transition from Norman to early English, with

capitals very beautifully carved by Mr J. H. Margeston of Bristol. The carving in the chancel, and those also of the chancel arch, are by the same hand, and all testify largely of the skill and taste of this rising artist... The Norman porch is entirely a restoration of the original structure – every stone of it having been carefully marked and numbered when taken down, and each carefully re-chiselled, and replaced on the restoration... Mr J. G. Picking had the superintendence of the works from its commencement."

The 20th century

Work in this century has included a statuette of St. Edward, designed by F. H. Newberry, erected on the east gable of the chancel in 1931, and work to the east end of the chancel and its north aisle in 1946 and 1947. This latter work involved blocking the north door of the aisle and inserting a new window above it, lowering the floor at the east end of the chancel to its former level, insertion of a new two-light window in each side wall and replacement of the former three-light east window by the present four-light one with embattled transome and intersecting tracery.

In the course of this work several interesting items came to light, including a fragment of painted plaster, three fragments of a Purbeck marble memorial slab and the long-lost grave slab of James Parkyn, rector, who died in 1702.

Creech
(St. John)

DURING THE 18th century when the building of 'follies' was fashionable, Denis Bond of Creech Grange – who had built the well-known Grange Arch on the Purbeck Hills – put the trend to more practical use by building this small church here in 1746 from materials recovered from the ruins of a former 12th century priory church at East Holme two and a half miles away.

The 12th century

The most significant old feature to be found in the present building is the splendid semi-circular headed chancel arch of two orders facing the nave. Both orders are carved with characteristic chevron and nail-head ornament and the jamb shafts, two on each side, have scalloped and foliage carved capitals and scalloped and

Chancel arch

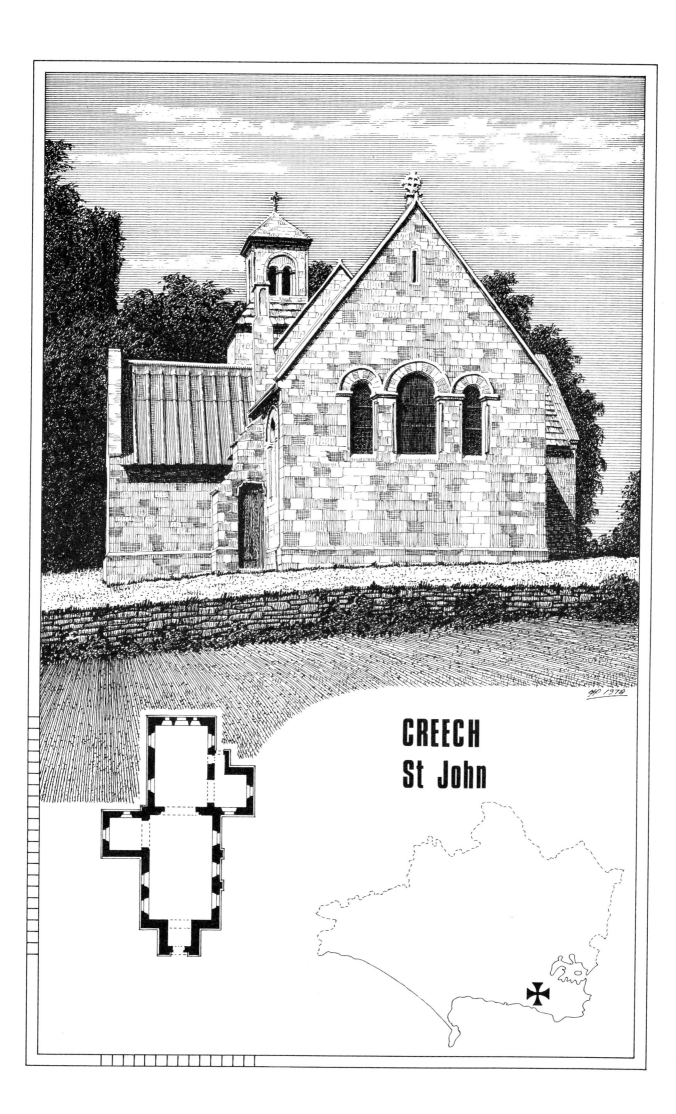

CREECH
St John

fluted bases which are, in fact, re-used inverted capitals.

Other 12th century features include parts of the tower arch, parts of the exterior of the west doorway, and parts of the internal nail-head ornamented string course below the wall plates of the chancel roof.

The 18th century

The building of 1746 incorporated the 12th century features referred to and comprised the present nave, with a south doorway, the lower parts of the west tower and a small chancel. Unfortunately, Denis Bond died whilst the work was under construction, so that it remained unfinished and was used as a carpenters' workshop for almost 100 years.

The 19th century

In 1840 John Bond continued the work of his ancestor and completed the building, as recorded in the stained glass of the east window of the chancel: "This chapel was fitted up at the expense of John Bond of Creech Esq., as a chapel of ease to the parish of Steeple AD 1840. He survived this good work only four years and died on March 18th 1844."

His brother and successor, the Rev. Nathaniel Bond, added the north transept in 1849, that date appearing in the stained glass of one of the windows, whilst the other is a memorial to his son and inscribed: "This aisle was erected for the use of the children of the Sunday School in affectionate remembrance of John, eldest son of Nathaniel Bond, Clerk and Mary his wife. He was born Nov. 17 1838 and died February 8th 1849." The windows themselves have plain jambs and architraved semi-circular heads, and as the two north windows of the nave are similar, they were probably inserted at the same time. The arch between the nave and transept, which has settled rather alarmingly on the west side, is decorated with chevron ornament and jamb shafts with scalloped capitals in Norman style. The transept roof has a segmental plaster ceiling divided into two bays by a segmental principal, similar to that of the nave which is in three bays.

Nathaniel Bond also added the elegant cupola to the west tower. It rises from a stone slated semi-pyramidal feature which may have been the original 'Purbeck type' tower roof and has, itself, a pyramidal roof, and pairs of semi-circular headed openings in each side. After these embellishments the chapel was consecrated in 1859.

In 1868 further alterations were carried out which included rebuilding the chancel to its present larger size, the addition of an organ chamber on the south side, removal of the south door of the nave to its present position in the west wall of the tower and the provision of three new windows in the south wall of the nave. Although some older work may have been re-used all the windows of this date are more elaborately detailed than the older ones. They are similar in shape and size but the jambs are enriched by exterior angle shafts with scalloped capitals, whilst the triple east window additionally has interior shafting. The roof, too, breaks with the simple plastered ceiling tradition of the earlier roofs, and is of barrel form divided into boarded panels by nail-head ornamented ribs. The organ chamber and chancel are accessible from outside by an unusual porch in the form of a wide two-stage buttress.

The influence of 12th century motifs was carried so far as to be somewhat inappropriately applied to timber fittings, where the organ chamber screen is of interlaced arcading decorated with nail-head ornament and shafts with scalloped capitals. The pulpit also is carved with interlaced arcading and the choir stalls are decorated with

nail-head ornament and angel finials.

The 20th century

Work during this century has included renewal of the pews in 1913, re-roofing the chancel and organ chamber in 1963-64 using asbestos cement Trafford tile sheeting, and the installation of electricity in 1966. Contrary to what might be expected, the asbestos sheeting has weathered to such an extent as to be unobtrusive though it is not a worthy substitute for the Purbeck stone slating it replaced and which still remains on the roofs of the nave and north transept.

East Burton
(no dedication)

FROM EARLY times what is now East Burton was an outlying part of Winfrith parish, and by the early 19th century a community had become established here and grown sufficiently to warrant the building of a chapel of ease. This proposal was reported in the Dorset County Chronicle of 31 January 1839:

"We have pleasure in calling the attention of our Church loving readers to the augmented list of contributions towards the erection of a Chapel at Burton, in the parish of Winfrith. We have been favoured with the sight of a plan of an elegant, chaste, and cheap church, which has been furnished gratuitously to the worthy vicar, by J. T. Parkinson, Esq., of Jersey, through the instrumentality of a lady who has taken considerable interest in this very desirable undertaking, which is, we trust, now about to be speedily carried into effect."

In fact, building work must have begun before the site was acquired, as the deed of conveyance of the land is dated 25 August 1840, less than a fortnight before the completed church was consecrated on 7 September.

The building is unusual in being orientated north-south, with the sanctuary at the north end rather than the east, but it is otherwise characteristic of the simple and unpretentious work of the early 19th century. The plan is a plain double-square rectangle with a porch at the south end, all with simple details. The walls are of stone rubble with Ham Hill dressings, divided into bays by single stage buttresses, and the windows are all of two-light form with elementary forked mullions, or Y tracery, under pointed heads. A blind pointed head recess in the north wall, a smaller four centre headed one in the south wall of the porch, and a blind quatrefoil near the apex of the main south wall are the only concessions to external embellishment which relieve otherwise plain gables.

The roof is slated, and the apex at the south end is carried over a timber framed and bracketed projection to form a bell housing, whilst internally there is a plastered ceiling at collar level with sloping soffites, divided into bays by queen post trusses where the feet of the queen posts are carved into pendants below the tie beams.

All the internal fittings were contemporary with the building itself, but the church having been declared redundant, they were removed in 1978 in the course of converting the premises into a harpsichord making workshop.

EAST BURTON

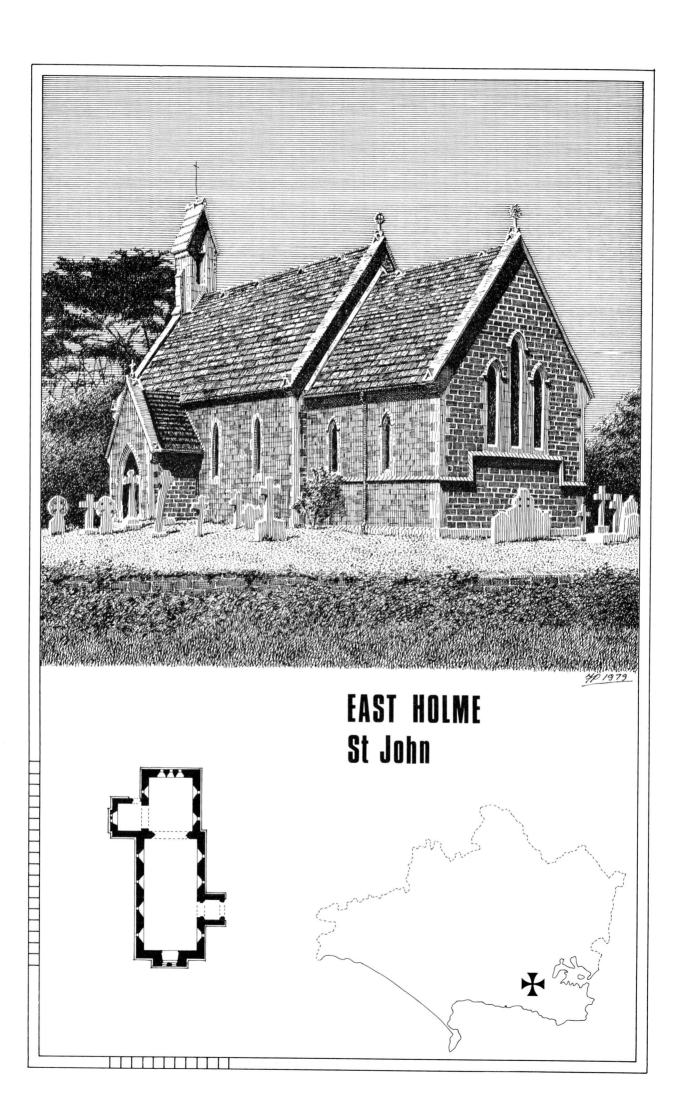

EAST HOLME
St John

East Holme
(St. John)

A CLUNIAC priory, under the jurisdiction of Montacute Abbey in Somerset, was founded here in the mid 12th century, and after the dissolution the priory church was retained and continued to fulfil a parochial function until 1715. In 1746 the mid 12th century chancel arch, a fine specimen of its time which must have formed part of the original building, was rescued from the ruins and re-used in building a new chapel at Creech Grange together with one or two other smaller features.

The remaining ruins, which stood just to the west of the present site, were finally cleared in 1865 when the new church was built, some of the old stone perhaps being re-used in the general walling work, which is of local brown heathstone, with Ham Hill dressings. Other fragments from the old priory are still preserved in the present church and churchyard, and include parts of a 13th century shaft and coffin lid, and fragments of 13th, 14th and 15th century window heads and cusping.

The present church was built in 1865-66 at the expense of Nathaniel Bond, as a memorial to his younger brother, as recorded on a carved stone frieze below the wall plates in the chancel – "This church is erected AD 1865 to the glory of God and in memory of Denis William Bond obiit January 23rd 1863." It was consecrated on 5 April 1866 and this ceremony and other details concerning the church are fully reported in the Dorset County Chronicle of 12 April 1866. The cost had exceeded £1500, "all of which has been paid by N. Bond, Esq."; the architect was John Hicks of Dorchester, and the builders Wellspring and Son of Dorchester.

The plan comprises a simple arrangement of chancel with a north vestry, and nave with a south porch and west gable bell-cote, all very similar in plan form and composition to Hicks' earlier church of 1861 at Athelhampton. At East Holme, however the style chosen is slightly earlier, being 'Early English' where the windows are mainly in the form of simple lancets – the east window being a graduated triplet, whilst the side windows of the chancel are trefoil headed. The chancel windows are further embellished internally by attached Purbeck marble shafting to the reveals. The west window is a paired lancet with a plate quatrefoil above, and occurs in a deep embrasure forming an external projection which supports the bell-cote. The south doorway has shafted jambs with foliage carved capitals.

Internally the chancel arch is pointed and moulded, and each respond has three attached Purbeck marble shafts with foliage carved capitals. The roofs of the chancel and nave, of open rafters below diagonal roof boarding, are divided into two and four bays respectively by arch braced principals supported on carved angel bust corbels in the chancel and short Purbeck marble shafts in the nave.

Illuminated texts occur over each window and the chancel arch, and these, according to the Chronicle, were painted by Lady Selina Bond. The oak pulpit, forming three sides of an octagon, is decorated by trefoil headed panels, and the font has a circular bowl ornamented with inserted alabaster emblems of the four evangelists, supported by trefoiled arcading on four Purbeck marble perimeter shafts clustered around a central circular stem.

In 1812, in the course of planting trees on the priory site, a memorial brass was unearthed, and subsequently fixed to the west wall of the present church in October 1907. It records Richard Sidwayne, gent, who died 2 November 1612, aged 63.

The following extract concerning the church and consecration day celebrations are taken from the Dorset County Chronicle of 12 April, 1866:

"We have again the pleasure of recording another act of private munificence, in the erection of a beautiful new church in the parish of East Holme, consecrated by the Lord Bishop of Salisbury on Thursday, an event which was the occasion of much rejoicing on the part of the inhabitants of the district, that will now be provided more adequately with the means of grace. The parish is small, and for a period of nearly 150 years has been dependent upon the neighbouring parish of Stoke for baptisms, marriages and burials. Though formerly the site of a considerable church, belonging to the abbey of Montacute, in Somersetshire, this had been pulled down and removed, and the tithes alienated. These defects have now been remedied through the liberality of the present owner of the estate, Nathaniel Bond, Esq., who has conveyed a piece of land, situated near his mansion, to the Ecclesiastical Commissioners, having enclosed it with a stone wall as a parish burying-ground, and in the centre of which he has built a little gem of ecclesiastical architecture, and re-endowed the church with the tithes of the parish.

"The building, which is in the early English style of architecture, was designed by John Hicks, Esq., of Dorchester, whose plans have been well carried out by Messrs. Wellspring and Son, builders, of Dorchester. It consists of a nave and chancel, with a vestry on the north and a porch on the south. The whole exterior walls are built with the red sandstone quarried on the estate, excepting the quoins and dressings of the windows, which are of stone from Ham Hill. The interior arches are of Bath and Ham Hill stone in alternate courses, having a very pleasing effect, and these rest upon columns of polished Purbeck marble... The details internal are wrought out most elaborately, and in a style which shows that no expense has been spared to make it worthy of the high purposes to which it is dedicated. Running round the interior is a bold cornice of Bath stone beautifully carved in floriated pattern; and the corbels in the nave have small Purbeck marble shafts terminating in bosses, some of them bearing shields, with coats of arms, being those of the ancient owners of the estate, commencing with that of Aldred de Lincoln, by whom it was conveyed to the Priory of Montacute, and terminating with the present owner. These, as well as the illuminated texts in other parts of the building, are the work of Lady Selina Bond, who has displayed great taste in this labour of love... As the stone fencing round the church-yard is sunk even with the surrounding park, the sacred edifice forms a beautiful object on this picturesque side of the Frome. The carved stone work was principally by Bolton, of Worcester, and the entire structure is a credit to all concerned. We believe the expense of the whole has exceeded £1,500, all of which has been paid by N. Bond, Esq., without application to any society or other person.

"In consequence of the smallness of the church, and Mr Bond's wish that all the parishioners should have the opportunity of being present at the consecration, and of hearing the Bishop's sermon, the attendance was restricted, as far as possible, to those, and a few only of the neighbouring clergy... The party of clergy and visitors were hospitably entertained at the mansion... The whole of the population of the parish were also hospitably entertained by the Squire, who had caused to be provided for them in the large barn, a plentiful dinner of roast beef and plum pudding. The Bishop paid a visit to the scene after the repast was concluded, and made a short speech, proposing the health of N. Bond, Esq., Lady Selina Bond, and their son and heir, which was warmly received. The weather was delightful throughout, and everything passed off in the most agreeable and satisfactory manner."

East Lulworth
(St. Andrew)

FEW CHURCHES can rival the magnificent setting of this one, situated in undulating and wooded rural parkland with the spectacular ruin of Lulworth Castle as a neighbour. However, the church itself has been rebuilt at least twice, in 1788 and again in 1864, so that the splendid 15th century west tower is now the only old structural feature remaining, although the church must have originated before then as known vicars are recorded from 1312.

Hutchins (1st edition: 1774) writing before the rebuilding of 1788, described the mediaeval building as consisting of "a chancel, a body and S. isle, and a small isle on the N. side of the chancel, all covered with lead. It has a very large embattled tower," and the editors of the second edition of 1796 add that: "The whole was a very ancient fabric, built in the style of the Norman architecture." However, this description cannot have been applicable to the tower, nor to the north wall of the nave, where in the words of the 3rd edition of 1861: "the jambs and sills of the Perpendicular windows still remain, as well as the jambs of the north doorway." The mediaeval north wall of the nave was evidently retained and incorporated into the 1788 rebuilding, and even in the present building the west end of this wall is largely original, and includes the 15th century casement moulded jambs, sill and part of the mullion of the north west window.

The 15th century

The tower is in four stages with boldly projecting diagonal buttresses of four receding stages to the eastern angles, and of five similar stages to the western ones. They extend to the base of the upper stage and end in pinnacled caps, above which the angles of the tower are chamfered. The parapet is embattled with pinnacles at the angles, and gargoyles below them on the parapet string which is additionally ornamented with paterae. The west doorway has a four centred head under a square label formed by a continuation of the plinth moulding, with blank shields in the spandrels. Unusually, instead of the normal west window, the ground stage has windows in the north, west and south walls, each of two cinquefoiled lights in square heads, that in the south wall being an insertion or renewal of 1864. The stair turret is contained wholly within the thickness of the north wall and north east angle without any external or internal projection.

The belfry windows are the most striking features which give this tower such an individual character. They are tall, well proportioned, deeply recessed, and arranged in groups of three to effectively dominate each face of the upper stage. Between the lights, at window head level, there are large, unusual and intriguing corbels, two on each face of the tower, and these must originally have supported the images referred to by Hutchins: "On each side were formerly the images of the four Evangelists; and on the W. side of the tower, St. John the Baptist."

Internally the ground stage of the tower must have been equally imposing, as the tower arch, although rather lower than normal and unusually triangular headed, is elaborately moulded on the nave side above a high plinth, and the jambs incorporate canopied niches which would originally have contained further images. Moreover the

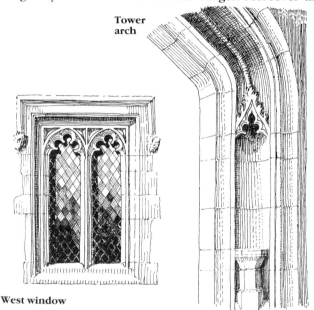

Tower arch

West window

ceiling seems originally to have been stone vaulted, as the springings in the form of angels holding shields still remain in each corner, with additionally parts of traceried pendants in the two eastern angles.

The font is also of the 15th century and of the usual octagonal form ornamented by sunken quatrefoil panels on the sides of the bowl, above a panelled stem.

The font

EAST LULWORTH
St Andrew

The 18th century

A royal coat of arms, formerly in the ground stage of the tower, but restored in 1973 and re-fixed in the chancel, is supported on a consoled bracket inscribed "THE GIFT OF THOS. WELD Esqr 1785" in old lettering re-gilded.

A faculty dated 31 July 1787 stated that the church was in a "ruinous & decayed" condition, and that it was proposed to take down the south aisle and the north aisle of the chancel, "And in lieu and stead thereof to erect in the West end of the said church an handsome Gallery of the length of Twenty feet and breadth of ten feet."

This work duly went ahead in 1788 and involved in addition the demolition of the former chancel and replacement by a semi-circular apse as shown on a later faculty plan. The old north wall of the nave seems largely to have been retained, but all the remainder, apart from the tower, must have been rebuilt. There were opposing north and south doorways, both with porches, that on the north side having been converted into a small vestry by 1863. According to the Dorset County Chronicle of 11 August 1864, the 18th century roof had been lead covered and of a low pitch (the outline of which can still be seen on the west wall of the nave) with a parapet all round, and internally there had been a segmental plastered ceiling.

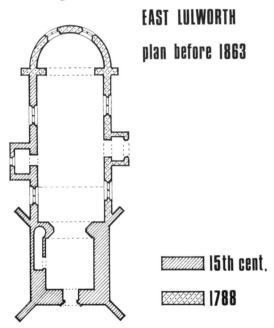

EAST LULWORTH

plan before 1863

15th cent.

1788

It is likely that the architect and builder was John Tasker who had designed and built the neighbouring catholic church for Thomas Weld in 1786-87, particularly as Mr Weld seems to have financed both projects. As Hutchins' editors (2nd edition: 1796) put it: "It was re-built in a neat and durable style by the present Mr Weld in 1788, previously to which, namely, June 11, 1787, he removed the coffins that were in the family vault under the church to the new catacombs he has made under the chapel, but left those under the pavement to remain as they were before."

If John Tasker was the architect, then judging by his work on the catholic church, that of 1788 on the parish church would have been of some distinction. Yet whilst the editors of Hutchins' 2nd edition of 1796 describe the building as being "in a neat and durable style", those of the 3rd edition of 1861 say: "There is nothing worthy of remembrance in the construction of the later portion of the edifice, as the architecture is a very mean character," showing the extent to which architectural taste had changed during the first half of the 19th century.

The 19th century

The organ is a tiny instrument of early 19th century date and has a mahogany case with pierced panelling.

In 1864 the whole building, except the tower, was rebuilt, the faculty being dated 1 August 1863, the estimated cost £580 (allowing for the value of old materials), and the architect John Hicks of Dorchester. According to the faculty document it had been intended to retain the nave walls in essence, and to insert new windows only, but in the event it seems that only parts of the north wall were retained. The portions of surviving 15th century windows seem to have prompted the selection of that period as a style for the new work, as the Dorset County Chronicle of 11 August 1864 says concerning them: "Happily, however, one or two were left, which afforded a key for the present restorations in the perpendicular style." Presumably the tower also must have been an influential factor.

The windows are all of vertical traceried type, and the chancel arch is of ogee-wave-ogee mouldings, the outer two being continued down the responds and the inner springing from attached shafts with foliage carved capitals. The roofs have plastered soffites between exposed rafters, that of the chancel being divided into two bays by pointed arch braced principals off foliage carved stone corbels, whilst the nave roof is divided into three main bays by four centre arch braced collar trusses off plain stone corbels, each bay being sub-divided by an unbraced sub-principal.

The church was re-opened for use at the end of July 1864 and the Chronicle, reporting this, says: "though any special ceremony in celebration of the event was, we understand, dispensed with." It goes on to describe the former building and the recent work, stating that Mr Wellspring of Dorchester had been the builder. Also that the vestry had been located on the site of the former north aisle of the chancel, and that: "In clearing away the ground the foundations of the old chancel were discovered and the new one has been carried out to the same extent."

At the time of the re-opening the bulk of the work had been completed, but there was by then a deficiency of funds, presumably due to the work having been more extensive than originally intended, and further funds were required to complete the work of providing chancel seating and a new ringing chamber floor.

East Stoke
(St. Mary)

THE FORMER mediaeval church was situated some way to the south west of the present church, in the meadows on the south side of the River Frome, seemingly rather remote from the village. Probably the site was originally one of pre-Christian significance, particularly as the churchyard appears to have been circular in shape, also, at the time of the domesday survey (1086) the river at this point formed the boundary between the hundreds of Bere and Winfrith, and hence probably also between comparable minster areas so that there may have been some particular reason for the church to have been built on the south side of the river in Winfrith Hundred.

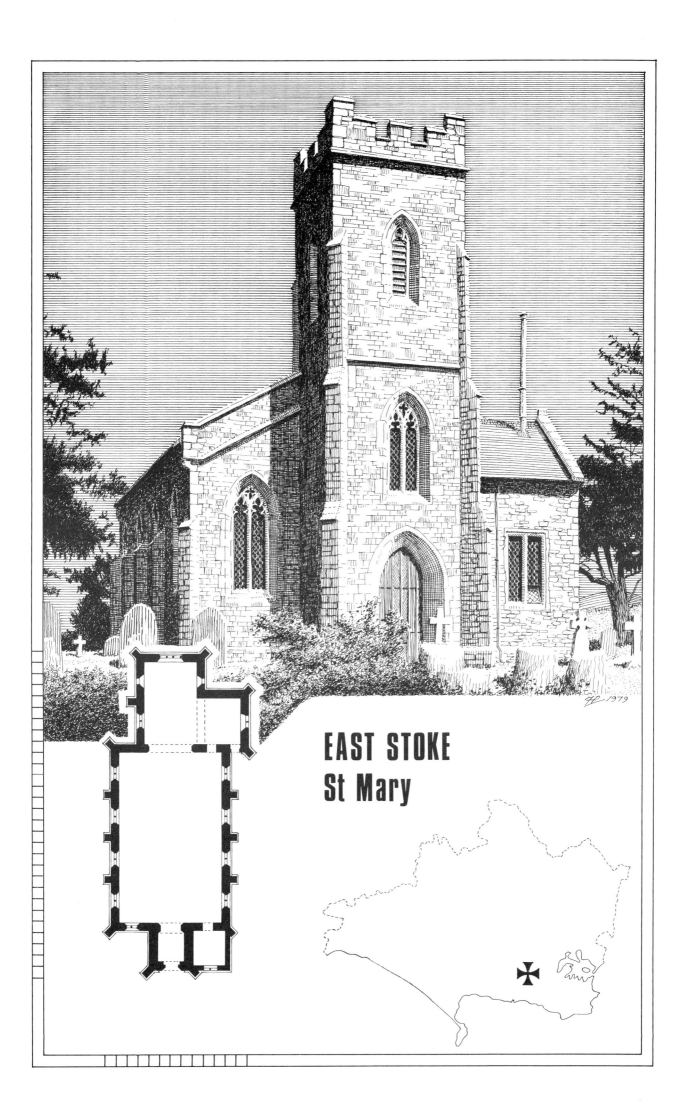

EAST STOKE
St Mary

The ruins still exist in the form of fragments of standing walls recognisable as parts of the south wall of the nave and a south porch, together with a few scattered and overgrown carved stones from arches and other features. These remains are now at the centre of a roughly circular copse representing the former churchyard, with ancient looking gravestones picturesquely interspersed among the undergrowth. Hutchins described the church as consisting of: "a body and chancel, both tiled, and a low tower, in which are three bells." It must have originated at least by the 13th century, as the font, now in the present church, is of that period. The bowl is hexagonal and was restored with some retooling, and mounted on its present stem and base in 1885 as recorded on a brass plate.

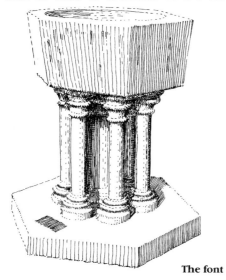

The font

Surviving architectural details among the ruins are mainly of 15th century date and include parts of a three light window in the south wall of the nave, voussoirs from the outer archway of the porch, and a very fine stoup on an engaged octagonal shaft against the east wall of the porch. The porch archway remained standing until the severe winter of 1963.

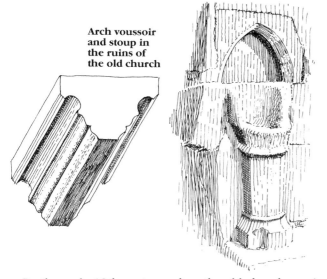

Arch voussoir and stoup in the ruins of the old church

By the early 19th century when the old church was in need of considerable repair, the possibility of rebuilding on a more convenient site was considered, and correspondence between the rector and Nathaniel Bond concerning this is preserved in the Dorset County Record Office (D 367/E49). When arrangements for a new site had been finalised, a printed statement appealing for additional subscribers was issued on 10 March 1828: "The situation of the Church, which stands in the Water-

Meadows between Wool and Holme Bridges is peculiarly low, and damp; and occasionally, when the adjoining Meadows are overflowed, not accessible to persons on foot without considerable inconvenience. It is moreover much too small, being capable of containing only 140 persons out of a population exceeding 500, and still increasing. For these reasons, in addition to its standing in need of considerable repairs, it cannot be rendered a commodious and decent place of worship, but at an expense greatly disproportionate to the little improvement its situation will admit of. It is therefore proposed to take down the present Church, and re-build it on a more dry, healthy, and convenient site, on the north side of the river near the high road... The expense can scarcely be calculated at less than £1500."

Work on the new church must have started soon afterwards, as the foundation stone laying ceremony was reported in the Dorset County Chronicle of 24 July 1828: "On Thursday, the Committee superintending the erection of the new church at East Stoke... with the subscribers and friends, met at the cottage of the Rev. Mr Butler, the Curate, in the afternoon, and partook of an excellent collation; after which they proceeded to the site of the intended building in the following order: – A band of music – upwards of 90 children belonging to the Sunday School – clergymen in their gowns – the architect (Mr Owen, of Portsmouth), with the plan, &c., – committee and gentlemen, two and two. On arriving at the ground, the children sang some appropriate verses of the 24th Psalm, and a very excellent prayer was delivered in a most impressive manner by Rev. C. Fox, the Rector. A plate, commemorative of the event, being then deposited, the foundation stone was laid by Miss Baine of Heffleton Lodge." Whilst the new church was being built the old one must have been taken down, as some of the old stone is said to have been re-used in the new building.

The church as then built consisted simply of a wide undivided nave, west tower and a small sanctuary projection at the east end, typical of new churches of that period, with equally characteristic and simple architectural details. Most of the original building remains intact, except for the sanctuary which has since been replaced by a larger chancel. The windows are of simple two light forked mullion or Y tracery type with cusping, and the original east window which is now in the north wall of the later chancel has ogee headed lights and vertical tracery. The bays of the nave are expressed externally by shallow single stage buttresses with diagonal ones of greater projection at the angles.

The tower is plain and not divided into external stages, except on the west face where there is a string course at about mid height above a west window and doorway flanked by three stage diagonal buttresses. The parapet is embattled, stepped up at angles, over a parapet string, and the belfry windows are single trefoil headed louvred lights. The tower arch is segmental and of one wide chamfered order continuous with the jambs. Internally the nave roof is divided into four bays by straight braced collar beam trusses, but in the original building of 1828 these were hidden by a shallow pitched plastered ceiling which followed the rake of the bracings, in the undersides of which the nail holes are still visible. All the original fittings have since been removed or replaced, but these are known to have included box pews and a west gallery, the staircase to which was in the north west corner of the nave against the west wall.

During later Victorian times when the Gothic revival movement was in full spate, churches built in the earlier part of the century were regarded with much disfavour, particularly on account of their small, or sometimes non-existent, chancels, and for their galleries and box pews which were in almost every church being replaced by the more popular open bench type pews. Such was the case here where a faculty dated 23 April 1885 described the church as having an "unecclesiastical appearance" due to there being no chancel, and to the presence of the west gallery of "unsightly appearance", and inconvenient pews. The work included the demolition of the original small sanctuary and replacement by the present chancel and organ chamber, removal of the west gallery, replacement of all the original seating, and removal of the plaster ceiling of the nave. The estimated cost was £850, and the architects were John Colson and Son of Winchester.

All the work is in typical Gothic revival form in marked contrast to that of 1828. The chancel arch is of three orders, the outer chamfer being continued down the responds, whilst the two inner mouldings spring from foliage carved corbels. The organ chamber is gabled to the south with a two light geometrical traceried south window, a shouldered doorway in the west wall and a shallow segmental pointed arch over the opening into the chancel. The east window of the chancel is of three lights with curvilinear tracery, supplemented by single light windows in each side wall of the eastern bay, and the roof is of exposed boarding between cross braced trussed rafters.

The work was completed before the end of the year, the official re-opening being reported in the Dorset County Chronicle of 26 November 1885. The builders were Beer and Son of Wareham, and evidently the cost had slightly exceeded the estimate given in the faculty document: "About £1000 has been raised by subscriptions, bazaar, &c., but a small debt still remains."

The south west vestry was added in 1912, the faculty being dated 25 October 1911, and the cost estimated at £50. No architect is referred to on the plans or faculty documents, and the vestry which is gabled to the south with a two light square headed window in the west wall, is somewhat awkwardly contrived to fill the space in the angle between the tower and nave at this point. It is now used to house equipment for a ducted warm air heating system.

The 12th century

The church now consists basically of a combined nave and chancel contained within a simple long rectangle, but the original Norman building, although of the same width, is likely to have been considerably shorter. Substantial parts of the west wall still remain in situ with the base of a buttress visible at the south west angle, together with the original south doorway which appears to have been centrally placed in the south wall, assuming it to still remain in its original position. It is fairly plain by 12th century standards, having a semi-circular, slightly elliptical head with a roll moulded edge and chamfered label above moulded imposts and roll moulded jambs.

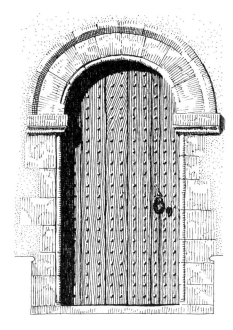

South
doorway

The rear arch is also semi-circular but stilted, and ornamented with a later painted scroll pattern thought to be of 16th century date. The original Norman font was discarded in favour of a new one during the 19th century, but in relatively recent times the old circular bowl was discovered lying in a nearby hedge, since when it has been reinstated and mounted on a modern stem and base.

Kimmeridge
(St. Nicholas)

THIS SMALL village of Purbeck stone and thatched cottages has probably not changed basically since Norman times when the church was first built here, retaining its original T-shaped layout with the manor house, church and vicarage grouped in a presiding position on the crossbar of the T at the upper end of the village street which threads its way down towards the sea. The church as it now stands is mostly of 19th century date, but the original Norman doorway still remains together with several other old features. This is one of the 16 or so mediaeval churches in Dorset without a dedication, or where the former dedication is unknown, but it has recently been dedicated to St Nicholas.

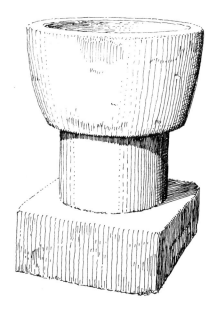

The
font

KIMMERIDGE
St Nicholas

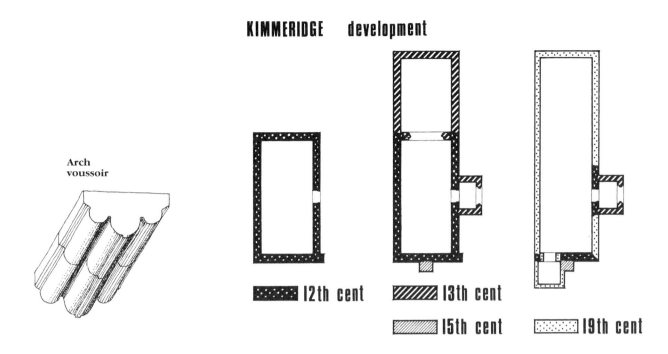

KIMMERIDGE development

Arch voussoir

▓▒▒▒ 12th cent   ▨▨▨ 13th cent

                             ▨▨▨ 15th cent   ▒▒▒ 19th cent

The 13th century

Before the 19th century the nave and chancel were structurally divided in a conventional manner by a chancel arch, and although this was taken out in the course of rebuilding work, many of the arch voussoirs still remain, lying loose in the churchyard and on the boundary wall near the entrance gate. They are of an unusual profile consisting of three roll mouldings, and of 13th century date, suggesting that a chancel might have been added at that time, extending the church eastwards to its present length. The south porch seems also to have been added or rebuilt at the same time, and still remains complete with a segmental pointed entrance arch of two continuous chamfers.

The 15th century

At this time a bell cote was added or rebuilt on the west gable probably specifically to house a new bell which itself still remains from the 15th century. The upper part of the bell cote has since been rebuilt, but the four centre headed bell aperture is original together with the associated buttress which was added centrally to the west gable wall. All the present windows are of the 19th century or later, but fragments of 15th century windows lying loose in the churchyard suggest that original small windows may have been at that time replaced by larger ones.

The 17th, 18th and 19th centuries

Apart from the early 17th century communion table, all the other old fittings have been swept away in the course of drastic 19th century restorations and rebuilding, but before that time it seems that the church had not been significantly altered since mediaeval times to judge by Hutchins' description (1st edition: 1774): "The Church is situate at the N. end of the parish, and consists of a nave and chancel. At the W. end is an arch, in which is one bell; the whole structure is small, plain, and very ancient; it is served once a fortnight by some neighbouring minister, appointed by the Clavells; it pleads exemption from episcopal or archidiaconal jurisdiction."

The vestry at the west end appears to have been an early 19th century addition, as the south window is a plain pointed single light characteristic of that period, and there are three further similar windows in the west wall of the nave, two of them at a high level which would presumably have been associated with a former west gallery. The gallery has since been removed, but there is still an unusual raised platform across the west end.

Apart from the west wall of the nave and the south porch and doorway, the whole of the remainder of the church was rebuilt later in the 19th century, much of it seemingly before 1860, as Hutchins' editors (3rd edition: 1861) include the statement that: "The windows are all modern, having been inserted a few years since in the place of small square ones, with wooden frames," ... and Sir Stephen Glynne, that indefatigable visitor of English churches who visited Kimmeridge on 1 August 1865, described it as: "A small church, almost totally rebuilt, and consisting merely of an oblong body including chancel, with a south porch and bellcot over the west gable." Further rebuilding is said to have been carried out in 1872.

The roof is at one continuous level and lined with diagonal boarding below the rafters with longitudinal ribs at the ridge and mid-points, and divided into one large and two smaller bays by unusual raking principals which incorporate two members on each side like raking newel posts which form the points of large cinquefoil cusping. They additionally have iron tie rods from the feet of the principals to central iron rings which are suspended from the apexes by further iron ties. Unusually there are no windows in the north wall of either the nave or chancel. The east window is of two trefoiled lights below a trefoiled roundel within a pointed head, and the south windows are each of two cinquefoil lights in a square head.

The south window west of the porch is later than the others, and the subject of a faculty dated 8 August 1912. It was to be inserted "where an old one has at some time been built up," and the estimate of £12. 15s 0d. from George Hardy of Swanage was "assuming that the old opening is inside as well as outside".

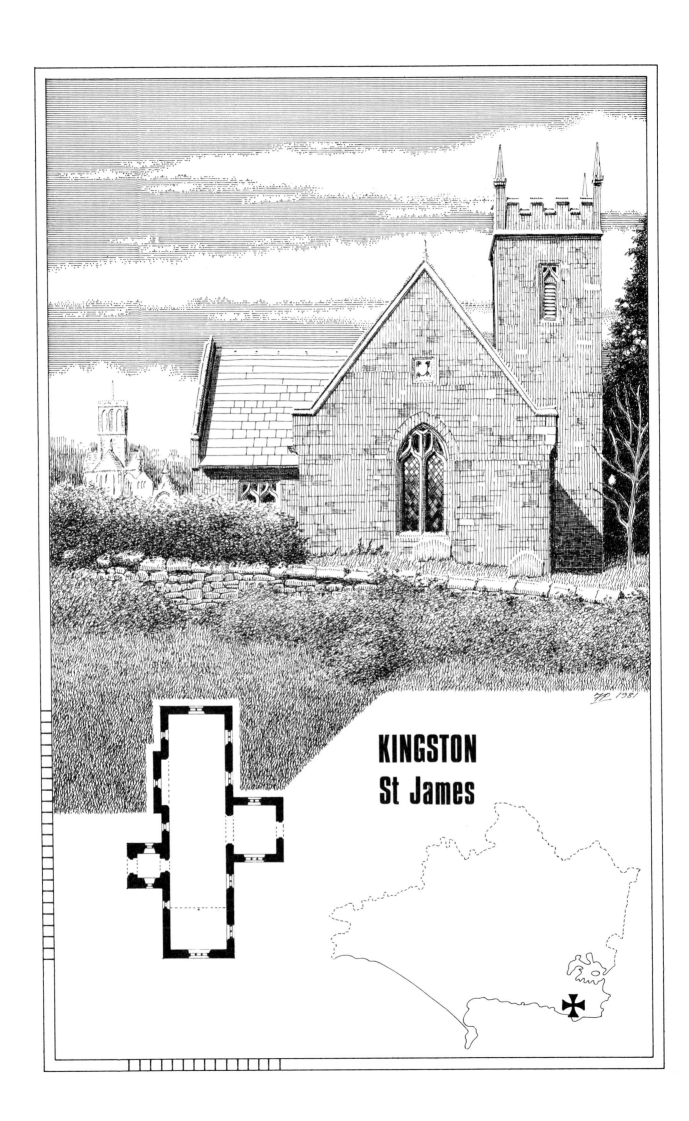

KINGSTON
St James

Kingston
(St. James)

HERE THERE are two churches, both conspicuously situated on high ground commanding extensive views, and lying within sight of each other on the east and west sides of the village. The older of the two, on the east side, although largely replaced by the later church in 1880, continued to be used for marriages and burials until 1921, since when it has served as a village hall, and after a spell of disuse was during 1979-81 converted into a dwelling. A church has existed on the old site since the 12th century, but the only remnant of this early building is now the semi-circular head of a Norman doorway carved with diaper ornament and reset flush into the west gable wall.

Norman door-head

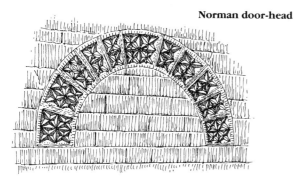

Kingston was a chapelry of Corfe Castle until 1877 when it became a separate ecclesiastical parish, and Hutchins (1st edition: 1774) says: "At the end of this hamlet is a small chapel dedicated to St James. It is officiated in by the rector of Corfe once a fortnight in summer, and once a month in winter" ... to which the second edition editors of 1796 add: "In consequence of an arrangement between William Morton Pitt esq., and the rev. Sir Thomas Bankes l'Anson, the rector of the parish in 1786, divine service has since that time been regularly performed once every Sunday in the year, for which extra duty Mr Pitt pays £15 per annum to the curate of the parish, but this arrangement is only to be in force during the good pleasure of the rector for the time being. The congregations have sometimes amounted to above 250 persons, so considerable a number seem well entitled to service every Sunday."

A scheme of total rebuilding was completed in 1833, but the former building seems to have been very much restored and a new tower added before then, as Sir Stephen Glynne who visited the church in 1830 wrote: "This church is of Norman origin, consisting only of a nave and chancel; but has been so completely modernized that very few traces of the original architecture are visible. A low modern tower is placed upon the north side. On the south side is the head of a Norman doorway now walled up, having a double band of toothed ornament. There is also a vestige of a plainer Norman door on the north of the chancel. The windows are all modern and of a wretched character. The interior is neatly pewed, but has scarce a vestige of antiquity."

According to DNHAS Proceedings (vol. 30, p lxxiii – lxxiv), in the 1870s there were still several old inhabitants who could remember the old church before being rebuilt: "There was a staircase outside that old chapel which led to a west gallery for the accommodation of a church band, and the band performed for a time after the new church had been built on the spot. The band was superceded by a barrel or grind organ."

The rebuilding is recorded on a stone plaque: "The very ancient chapel which stood in this place being much decayed this Chapel the building of which was completed in the year 1833 was erected at the sole expense of John Scott, first Earl of Eldon, also Viscount Encombe and Baron Eldon." The Earl's son-in-law George Repton was the architect, and the builder was John Tulloch of Wimborne, according to the Dorset County Chronicle of 15 August 1833, which in its report on the commencement of rebuilding at Lytchett Minster, refers to "Mr John Tulloch of Wimborne, who has recently built the Churches of Hamworthy, Kingston and Parkstone".

Some of the walls are no doubt built on the foundations of the older building, and the plan comprises a combined nave and chancel, south transept and north tower, the lower storey of which formed a north entrance porch in addition to a direct entrance in the south wall of the south transept. The whole building is in the severe and plain early Gothic revival style prevalent in the 1830s, with double pitched slated roofs having conventional eaves and parapetted gables with kneelers, and windows of uncusped ogee headed lights, mostly in square heads with glazed spandrels, but the main east and west windows have uncusped vertical tracery in a pointed and four centred head respectively. The tower is equally plain

A lithograph of 1844 showing the old church from the south west. Evidently the south transept did not exist at that time and must have been a subsequent addition to the rebuilding of 1833

without either buttresses or dividing strings, with an embattled parapet and obelisk shaped pinnacles at the angles, and the belfry windows, which occur in each face except the south, are of single ogee headed louvred lights with open spandrels in square heads.

There is a faculty dated 16 September 1880 for a restoration of seats and fittings and removal of the west gallery, the architect being G. E. Street R.A. of London, who had designed the new church completed shortly before. In the event the gallery was not at that time removed as it remained until the recent works of conversion into a dwelling.

In 1874 work began on building an entirely new church on a new site on the west side of the village, all at the expense of Lord Eldon, and when completed in 1880 it became to all intents and purposes the new parish church, replacing the old one. At the same time, although dedicated on 24 July 1880, it remained in the ownership of Lord Eldon, and was not therefore officially considered a parish church as such, so that marriages and burials still continued to take place at the old church.

The architect was G. E. Street (1824-81), and this must have been one of his last works which he is said to have considered his best. It is certainly a fine and impressive building with an air of grandeur unexpected in such a quiet corner of Dorset, deriving from a combination of town church scale, cathedral-like proportions and composition, and a rural village context. Nevertheless as far as materials and workmanship are concerned it could hardly be more local, as in the words of the Dorset County Chronicle of 29 July 1880: "The stone has all been quarried on Lord Eldon's estate; the marble has all been raised from a quarry opened for the purpose close to the church, whilst the oak for the roofs and the stone slates with which they are covered have been brought from his lordship's Gloucestershire estate at Stowell."

The workmanship is of an exceptionally high standard, particularly since most of it is by the Encombe estate workers, who although probably well versed in the use of Purbeck stone, are unlikely to have been experienced in the construction of arches and vaulting, and in the other specialised techniques involved. Again to quote the County Chronicle: "This noble church has now been completed after some six years of hard work. The whole has been erected without the aid of contractors by Lord Eldon's own men under the admirable direction of Mr Elder as clerk of the works. Mr G. E. Street, R.A., the architect, has designed every detail of the fabric and fittings, and has evidently had the rare satisfaction of being allowed to do everything in the best possible way. He has, indeed, designed and seen carried out a very handsome cathedral-like structure, and he may well be congratulated on the results."

The plan consists of an apsidal chancel with a two storeyed vestry wing on the north side, central crossing tower with transepts, nave and aisles, and a west entrance porch in the form of a narthex with opposing north and south entrances and a seven bay arcaded range of windows in its west wall. The details throughout are consistently in Street's characteristic 13th century idiom, with lancet windows in singles, pairs and triplets, mostly with internal shafting, except in the west gable of the nave where there is a large traceried circular window. The central tower separates and soars above the roofs of the nave, chancel and transepts, with triple arcades of lancets in the upper stages, all three being louvred openings in the west face, but in the form of one louvred opening flanked by two blind arches on the remaining sides. The two additional louvred openings on the west face of the belfry stage were presumably provided so that the bells could be more readily heard at Lord Eldon's house at Encombe a mile away to the south west. There are square set buttresses at the angles below the upper stage, and the parapet is plain and weathered above a dentilled string course. The stair turret rises at the north east corner of the north transept, away from the tower itself, and continues above roof level as a free-standing circular turret with a conical roof, and its walls ornamented with arcading and a diaper pattern similar to that on a turret at Christchurch priory from which it is said to have been copied.

The interior is perhaps even more impressive than the exterior, where the cathedral-like effect seems to be enhanced in scale through being enclosed, and by the authentic use of 13th century details and lavish amounts of Purbeck marble shafting, particularly on the arcade piers. These are in clusters of eight with foliage carved stone capitals supporting finely moulded pointed arches with dog-tooth ornament to the central orders and Purbeck marble labels on the nave side. Similar but larger clustered Purbeck marble shafted responds and moulded arches span each side of the crossing in association with vaulting shafts which rise to support the springing of ribbed stone vaulting over the crossing, transepts, chancel and apse, producing a more lavish effect at the east end of the church in contrast to the open timber roofs of the nave and the aisles. These are of exposed rafters and boarding, of lean-to form over the aisles, with the double pitched roof of the nave divided into bays by arch braced principals.

Interior of the 1874-80 church showing the cathedral-like proportions and general effect
[Photograph: Colin Graham]

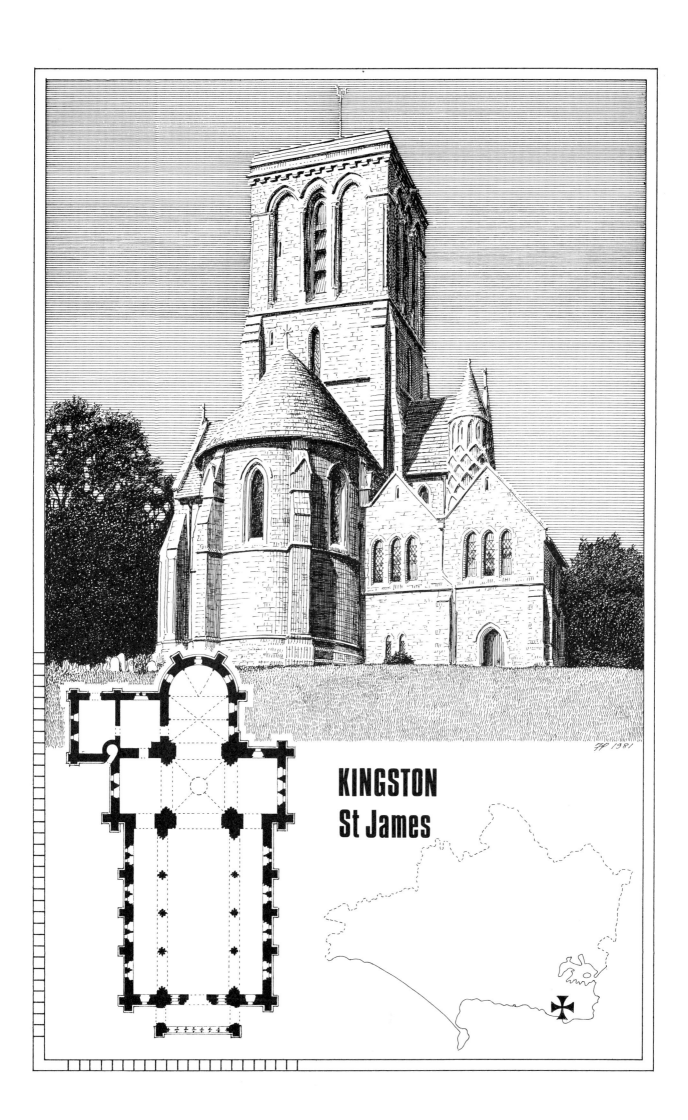

KINGSTON
St James

Street was renowned for his use of wrought ironwork, and here he was able to exploit this material to its full potential not only in the form of intricate door hinges and fittings, but in a large and elaborate chancel screen and a remarkable openwork wrought iron pulpit. As stated by the County Chronicle, all other fittings and furnishings were designed by Street, all producing a consistent and cohesive effect related to the structure itself, and the church was also provided with a large organ, by Maley, Young and Oldknow of London, and a full peal of eight bells. In fact no effort or expense seems to have been spared throughout the building – Street himself made clay models of the foliate capitals from which the carver, Milburn of York, worked, and the total cost of the whole church is said to have been in the region of £60,000 – an extraordinarily high sum by 1880 standards.

In April 1921, over forty years after it had been completed, the church and churchyard were conveyed to the Church Commissioners for the use of the parish, and consecrated as such on 11 October 1921. As stated in the Dorset County Chronicle of 20 October 1921: "In 1880 the late Bishop Moberly dedicated the church, and it has been used regularly for divine service since that time, but was not consecrated until now." Following this consecration it officially became the parish church in place of the old one on 19 January 1922.

Langton Matravers
(St. George)

DURING THE 19th century this church was rebuilt twice – in 1828 and again in 1875-76, on both occasions with the exception of the tower which is now the only old structural feature remaining. The former mediaeval church must have originated at least by the early 13th century, as the advowson, or presentation to the living of the church, is referred to in an assize roll of 1214. The font, of later 13th century date, is octagonal with a pair of trefoil headed panels in each side of the bowl, which is supported by an octagonal stem having eight attached perimeter shafts on a renewed octagonal base. Hutchins

The font

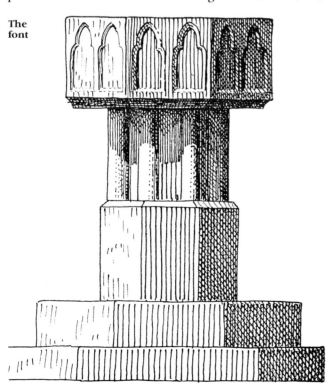

(1st edition: 1774) wrote of the old building: "The Church of Langton Matravers stands near the W. end of the parish. It is an ancient building, consisting of a chancel, body, and two isles, whereof the N. is a small one, belonging to Wilkswood farm, and was probably a chapel, made use of by that priory: the S. isle is of equal length with the body of the church. The whole fabric is tiled; the tower is embattled, and has in it three bells. There is an aperture in the wall that divides the body from the chancel. The dedication is uncertain, but by the presentation of Henry Attechappele to the chantry, it seems to be dedicated to St George, or at least the N. isle where the chantry was; or it might be dedicated to St Leonard, as the priory was."

The tower itself is of 15th century date, but the tower arch, which is small and more like a doorway, is of two wave moulded orders characteristic of 14th century work. The size of the arch would have been governed by the height of the older nave to which the tower was at first added, and the outline of this lower and narrower nave roof can still be seen above the tower arch. The tower is of two stages with diagonal buttresses at the western angles of the lower stage, an embattled parapet, and three belfry windows each of two trefoiled lights in a square head. A fourth belfry window in the east face was blocked in 1828 to accommodate a higher nave roof, the outline of which still remains visible internally between the mediaeval roof line and the present roof of 1875-76. The original square stair turret at the south east angle was rebuilt to its present octagonal form in the same position as part of the 1875-76 rebuilding, before which time, according to the faculty plan, it projected irregularly into the nave. The 15th century casement moulded jambs and square head of the west window remain, but the mullions and sill have been removed, probably in 1828, and the opening extended to ground level to form a door and fanlight arrangement.

The only other mediaeval remains are a pair of head stops reset on either side of the west window, presumably the former external label terminations, a former gable cross now reset above the south doorway, and one of the bells which is of early 15th century date. A 16th century carved oak panel which depicts St George and the dragon is probably of European origin, and a brass plate beneath it records: "In memory of John Ainscow Dugdale Captain, the Norfolk Regiment 1893-1919. Presented by his brothers." A brass plate of 1630, now on the east wall of the nave, records the deaths of three members of the Havelland family of Wilkswood – John (1607), his wife Mary (1587), and their son Thomas (1624), and is of interest for having been missing for 100 years. It is recorded in the first two editions of Hutchins (1774 and 1796) but is not referred to in the third edition of 1861, so that it probably disappeared during the rebuilding of 1828. However, it was discovered in the vicarage at Tollesbury in Essex in 1927, and was returned to Langton church in 1928 by Hugh de Havilland of Great Horkesley, Essex. In Hutchins' time it had been fixed to the south wall of the chancel within the communion rails, and included a Havelland shield of arms at the top, but this and the left hand edge of the inscription are now missing.

According to a faculty dated 1 June 1828 the church had by then become in a "very dilapidated and ruinous state and is so ill suited to the accommodation of the increasing population of this parish," and approval was sought "authorising the taking down of Langton Matravers Church, and rebuilding the same". A plan of the 1828 church is included with the later faculty drawings of 1875, and shows it to have consisted of a characteristic

LANGTON MATRAVERS
St George

wide aisleless nave with a small three sided apse at the east end. There was an east window, three windows in the north wall of the nave, and two on the south side flanking a central south doorway and porch, all of two lights, and no doubt all with simple Y tracery. The nave was slightly longer than at present, and was built considerably off centre relative to the tower, occupying the position of the present nave and south aisle combined, and of almost that width, to the extent that the outside faces of the 1828 nave walls coincided with the inside faces of the present north arcade and south wall of the south aisle. There was a small vestry on the north side of the apse, and on the faculty plan this is shown in dotted outline only and labelled: "site of vestry fallen down". Altogether the former building must have been typical of the plain churches built during the late 1820s and 1830s which were so much disliked later in the century when Hutchins' editors (3rd edition: 1861) predictably stated: "This edifice, with the exception of the tower, was taken down in 1828, and rebuilt with nave, chancel and south porch in a style which lays but little claim to architectural propriety."

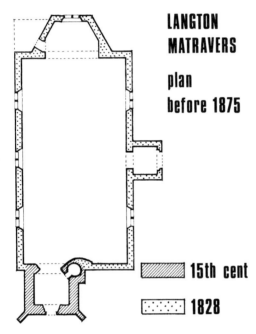

LANGTON MATRAVERS

plan

before 1875

▨ **15th cent**

▦ **1828**

Less than 50 years later the church was said to have been again in a state of "general decay and in an unsafe condition," so that the faculty dated 4 February 1875 was for complete rebuilding, again retaining the old tower. The estimated cost was £3500, and the architect was G. R. Crickmay. The scheme as proposed envisaged considerable remodelling of the tower, which would have included strengthening the existing two stages by the provision of square set buttresses at the angles in place of the diagonal ones, and increasing its height by the addition of a third stage. However, this part of the work was not in the end carried out, leaving the old tower as it stood to be dwarfed by the rest of the building, to the extent that the height of the new nave roof actually exceeded that of the old tower.

The rebuilding scheme resulted in a considerable enlargement over the previous church to comprise a nave with full length aisles, and chancel with a symmetrical arrangement of north organ chamber and south chapel, all in pseudo 13th century style. The east window is of three widely spaced graduated trefoiled lancets with quatrefoil tracery in the upper part of the centre light, complete with a graduated external label and internal shafting, whilst the remaining three light windows, in the north

and south walls of the aisles, are each of three graduated trefoiled lights under pointed heads with trefoiled roundels in the spandrels. The west windows of the aisles and the east window of the organ chamber are each of two trefoiled lights with a quatrefoiled roundel within a pointed head, but the east window of the south chapel is of two trefoiled lancets with a separate trefoiled circular window above them. There are also single trefoiled lancets in the side walls of the chancel and south chapel, and a pair of similar lights in the north wall of the organ chamber. The clerestory windows are also trefoiled lancets.

All the internal archways are pointed, with various combinations of 13th century mouldings, the chancel arch being of two keel moulded orders, the outer continued down the responds and the inner springing from short marble attached shafts with foliage carved stone capitals and corbels. On the north and south sides of the chancel there are two bay arcades to the organ chamber and south chapel, having arches with outer hollow chamfers and inner keel mouldings supported by Purbeck marble cylindrical columns, and responds in the form of pairs of similar but more slender columns, all with foliage carved stone capitals, and stone neck mouldings at mid-height on the columns. The arches at the east ends of the aisles are each of one wave moulded order, whilst those in the arcades are of two chamfered orders springing from short cylindrical columns with high octagonal to near square splayed bases, and octagonal capitals with bands left roughly tooled for carving which has never been carried out.

The roofs of the aisles are of low pitch lean-to form, each divided into twelve bays of three panels by moulded intersecting beams, in three main structural bays marked by heavier principals carried on braced wall posts above quadrant shaped stone corbels. All the other roofs are of double pitched form in exposed rafters and boarding, that of the chancel being to a four sided polygonal profile and divided into three bays by arch braced principals. Over the organ chamber and south chapel the roofs are of open trussed rafters, and the more elaborate nave roof is divided into four bays by arch braced collar trusses with braced hammer beams and iron tie rods, supported by marble wall shafts with moulded capitals and bases above flared stone corbels which occur in the arch spandrels. Each bay is sub-divided by a secondary braced principal.

Kelly's directory of 1895 states that the 1875-76 rebuilding had cost £4800, and it is evident that the work was curtailed through lack of funds in the latter stages. The tower was not heightened as intended, the nave arcade capitals were left uncarved, and a large stone in the east wall of the chancel externally, presumably intended as a commemorative plaque was left blank. This is borne out by the fact that when the new church at nearby Kingston was dedicated on 24 July 1880, "the offertory, which amounted to £25. 10s. 9d., was given towards the fund for liquidating the debt on Langton church." Although the debt must have been eventually paid off the unfinished items were never completed, but a faculty dated 14 August 1908 was for the provision of an oak reredos and panelling to the east wall of the chancel.

The completion of the rebuilding was reported in the Dorset County Chronicle of 26 October, 1876: "Its rebuilt and now handsome church ... which on Wednesday week was opened for Divine service, is, however, well worth a visit, if only for the sake of seeing an admirable specimen of ecclesiastical architecture, modern though it is. The edifice as it previously existed was long a grievous eyesore; it was, in fact, to quote from an admirable little work of a learned typographer of the district, a most miserable specimen of that ecclesiastical architecture in fashion fifty years ago... and the work in hand having been entrusted to the superintendance of Mr G. R. Crickmay, of Weymouth, diocesan architect, there was every prospect of a successful consummation. The latter gentleman has distinguished himself in the restoration of the sacred buildings in our diocese, and has certainly provided a very creditable substitute for the former church at Langton Matravers... On the site of the new edifice three churches have stood within 50 years. In 1828 the original structure was still in existence, but, being in a dilapidated condition and deficient for the increasing wants of the parish, it was demolished with the exception of the tower, and a square barn like building was erected in its stead in the most debased style of that period without the least pretence to architecture. Constructed, however, without arch or other support, the roof proved too strong for the wide span and soon began to push the walls out of the perpendicular. Cracks were the consequence, which from time to time were filled up with cement and other material, but at length daylight was visible through so many yawning fissures and the plaster was so frequently falling in large lumps to the ground... The new building is in the Early Geometric period of Gothic architecture in vogue in the latter part of the 13th century... The caps and bases of the columns throughout are left rough and boasted for the carving, which will be executed, and the remaining work will be completed as soon as some kind friends come forward and contribute towards the furnishings." The work was carried out by "Mr Thomas Gerrard acting as clerk of the works and builder".

Sandford
(St. Martin)

SANDFORD IS not strictly speaking within the Purbeck area but it lies in the large rural parish of Wareham St Martin which extends north of the town and represents the remains of the Domesday hundred of Charborough. This hundred probably approximated to the minster area served by the Saxon church of Wareham St Martin, so that this parish, which includes Sandford, has been closely tied to Wareham ecclesiastically for well over 900 years. Sandford itself is of relatively recent origin, owing its growth during the 19th century to the pottery industry. Hutchins (1st edition: 1774) referred to it as: "Sandford, two or three houses, a mile N.E. from Wareham".

The church, or more correctly the parochial chapel, is unusually situated in the grounds of Sandford St Martin C.E. First School to which it is physically attached with a communicating door from the school entrance hall. This is because for much of its life the building was the school, serving a dual role when it was used as a church on Sundays, and commonly referred to either as Sandford school or Sandford chapel. There is no reference to a school here in Kelly's directory for 1875, but it is first referred to in the directory for 1880 when the mistress

was Miss Emily Taylor, and the directory for 1885 states that it had been built "about 1875". The 1903 directory appears to be more specific, describing the school as "Elementary, Sandford, built in 1877, the gift of the late Mr Rodgett," ... but it must have been built before 1877 as the Dorset County Chronicle of 21 December 1876 reported: "On Thursday last a pleasing entertainment was given in the schoolroom at Sandford."

Miles Rodgett, J.P. of Sandford House was one of the principal landowners in the Wareham area, and after his death on 6 June 1882, his widow presented a new organ to the church of Wareham St Mary as a memorial to him. The Dorset County Chronicle of 31 May 1883, reporting on the dedication service of the memorial organ, observed that Miles Rodgett had been "a devoted admirer of all that appertained to church music, and himself an accomplished performer on the organ, having erected a fine instrument in Sandford Chapel at his own expense, and in which he took great delight."

At first the school or chapel consisted only of the main block orientated on an east-west axis forming the nave of the present church. This is rectangular on plan with gables at each end and divided into six structural bays expressed externally by buttresses and internally by arch braced roof trusses supporting a steeply pitched roof of exposed boarding and rafters. Externally the walls are faced with locally made buff bricks with stone dressings, and the roof is slated.

When Miles Rodgett initiated and financed the building he presumably envisaged the installation of a large organ in view of the unusually steep pitched roof. The organ is remarkably large for such a small building occupying rather more than the whole of the western bay, filling the space completely with ranks of pipes extending up to and following the steep profile of the roof. It has three manuals and was built by Maley, Young and Oldknow of London, the same firm who built the organ at Kingston church in 1880 and the memorial organ at Wareham St Mary, already referred to, in 1883.

The north wing was added as a separate infants classroom in 1892 according to Kelly's directory for 1899, and although it generally matches the earlier part, the bricks are of a different size and do not course with the earlier ones causing a straight joint to occur at the abutments. The projecting sanctuary at the east end is also of differing sized bricks and is evidently also a subsequent addition, having a distinctive east window of three graduated square headed lights divided into square panes, six of which are in coloured glass producing the effect of a cross. Internally the sanctuary is divided from the nave by a lightly chamfered pointed arch, the angles of the jambs being formed in beaded fashion by embedded slender cast iron columns having half octagonal capitals with foliage and egg-and-dart decoration.

Evidently the school was intended to serve also as a church from the time it was first built, in view of the organ and the County Chronicle's reference to 'Sandford Chapel' in 1883, and by 1903 it was regarded as a recognized place of worship, as under that heading Kelly's directory for that year states: "A service is held every Sunday in the school at Sandford by the Wareham clergy." The school was enlarged to the south in 1957, and following further extensions the original part of the building has since 1966 or 1967 been used solely as a church. The church is licensed for services, but has never been consecrated as such. The former infants wing on the north side is now a useful multi purpose room used variously as a vestry, general meeting room, refreshment area, parish room and for a local playgroup.

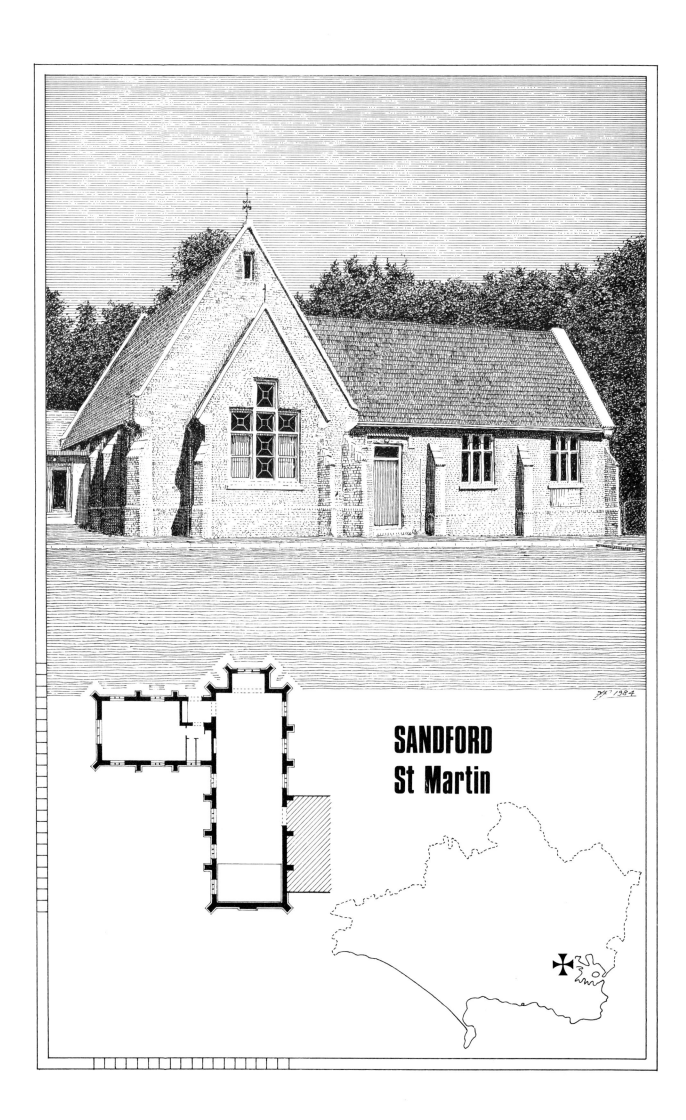

SANDFORD St Martin

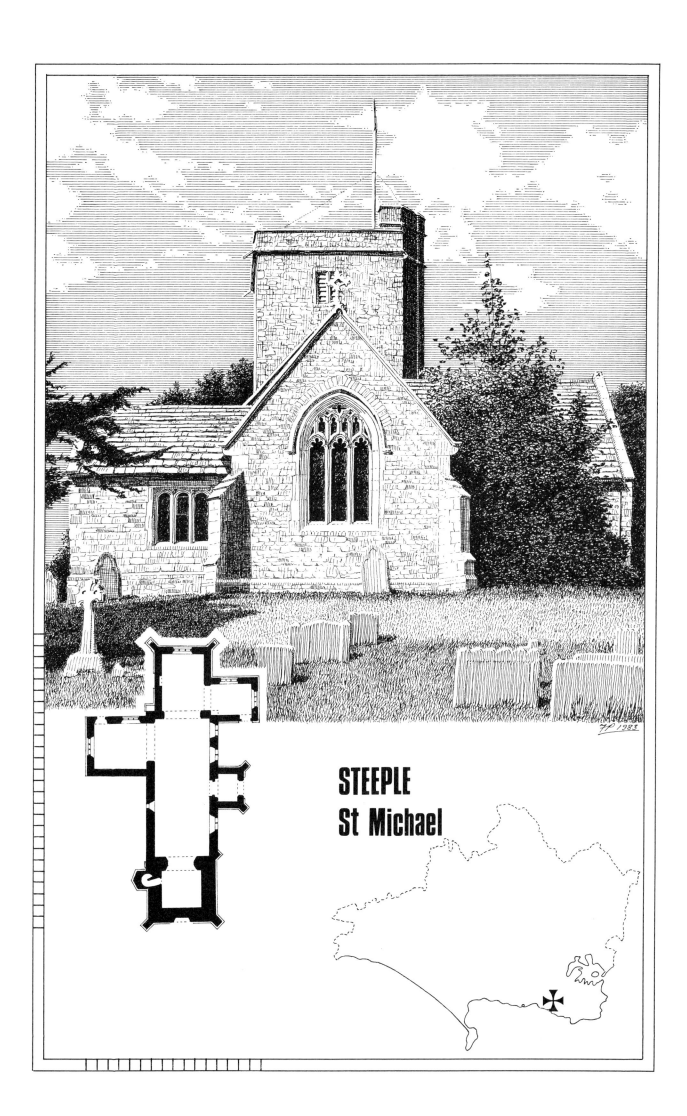

STEEPLE
St Michael

STEEPLE development

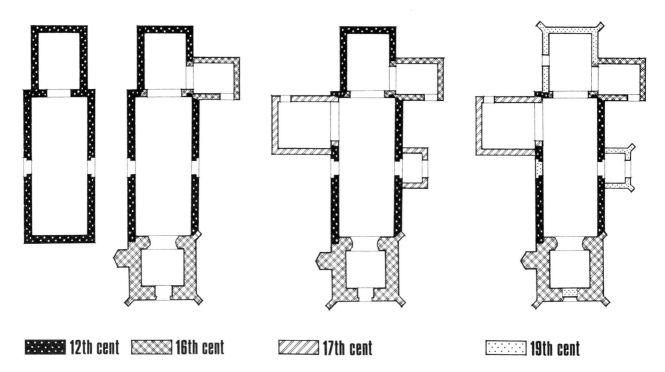

| ▨ 12th cent | ▧ 16th cent | ▨ 17th cent | ⬚ 19th cent |

Steeple
(St. Michael)

THIS CHURCH is of particular interest to American visitors, for here in this typically rural part of Purbeck are to be found unexpected links with George Washington, first President of the United States. The Lawrence family, who had married into the Washington family, ancestors of George Washington, in the 14th century, moved to Steeple and Creech Grange in 1540, living there until that branch of the family became extinct in 1691, when Creech Grange was sold to the Bond family, the present owners. Edward Lawrence financed various enlargements and alterations to Steeple church in the 17th century, and his arms which appear on the north transept, nave roof and porch, are, in heraldic terms – Quarterly, 1 and 4, argent a cross ragulé gules (Lawrence); 2 and 3, argent two bars and in chief three mullets gules (Washington): a crescent gules for difference. As the Washington component of the arms could be described as a 'Stars and Stripes' motif, it is thought possible that this may have influenced the design of the United States flag.

Lawrence arms

The 12th century

The church originated in the 12th century, and much of the original nave walling still survives, to include the chamfered plinth of a clasping buttress which marked the north west angle and opposing north and south doorways. The north doorway, with lintel and rounded arch has since been blocked, and the south doorway, although restored and largely rebuilt in the 19th century, retains its

South door-way

original form and materials. By Norman standards it is a simple one, having a semi-circular head of two lightly chamfered orders with similar jambs and hollow chamfered imposts. The chancel arch was rebuilt, probably to the same dimensions as before on the original foundations, and the chamfered plinths on either side of the original chancel arch still remain at the east end of the nave.

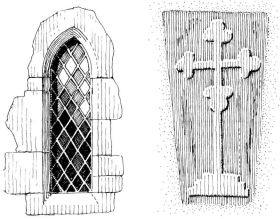

Lancet window and coffin lid

The 13th century

The principal items of this period are a lancet window in the north wall of the nave, and the font which consists of a plain circular tapering bowl and circular stem on a later octagonal base. An interesting coffin lid carved with a raised trefoiled cross on a stepped calvary base, now reset on the north wall of the chancel, is unusually small and probably originally covered the grave of a child or a heart burial. There is another coffin lid of similar date carved with a foliated cross on a stepped calvary in the churchyard south of the porch.

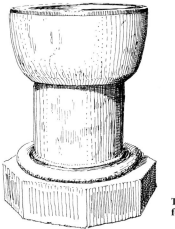

The font

The 15th century

No significant structural enlargements or alterations appear to have taken place during this period, but three new windows were inserted in the south wall of the nave, no doubt to replace very much smaller original ones.

15th century window

They are each of two cinquefoiled lights in a square head, but they all differ in detail – the eastern window has an outer chamfered surround, the central one has no outer moulding at all, whilst the most westerly window has an outer casement moulding. Internally, two quadrant shaped stone corbels flanking the most easterly of these three windows may have been the former rood beam corbels reset in this position.

The 16th century

Early in the 16th century the west tower was added. It is of two external stages with a plain parapet, diagonal two stage buttresses at the western angles, and an unusual projecting stair turret on the north side which rises above the general parapet level. The pointed west door has since been blocked, whilst the west window above it is a subsequent replacement or insertion. The belfry windows are each of two square headed lights filled with stone louvres, and internally the pointed tower arch is of one wide continuous chamfer. One of the bells, inscribed 'Sancte Anne Ora Pro Nobis' is of early 16th century date and probably contemporary with the tower itself.

The chapel on the south side of the chancel was added probably late in the 16th century. It opens to the chancel by a pointed and lightly chamfered arch, the east and south windows are each of three cinquefoiled lights with shallow cusping in square heads, and the external door in the west wall has moulded jambs and a segmental head formed out of a single block of stone below a relieving arch. The chancel arch, of high four centre profile, has similar continuous chamfers to those of the south chapel arch and is probably of similar date.

The south chapel formerly belonged to the Bonds of Blackmanston, and Hutchins (1st edition: 1774) says concerning William Bond: "This manor was conveyed to him in 1613... He lived at Blackmanston 82 years; and was buried in Steeple church in Blackmanston isle, 1636, in a window of which were his arms," and the editors of the 3rd edition of 1861 add that the aisle had probably been built by him. As the chapel or aisle seems to have been already in existence at the time of William Bond's death in 1636, it had presumably been built at some earlier period during his lifetime.

The 17th century

The north transept was added by Edward Lawrence in 1616, as a stone panel above the east door is carved with the Lawrence and Washington quartered arms with that date and initials E.L. The doorway itself has chamfered jambs and a four centre head with sunk spandrels in a square outer head, and the three-light windows have square headed lights in the north wall and four centre headed ones in the east wall. The transept opens from the nave by a pointed arch of two orders, the outer continuous, plain and plastered, and the inner of stone and chamfered springing from shaped and moulded stone corbels.

The former porch was probably also added or rebuilt at about the same time, as Hutchins' editors (3rd edition: 1861) say: "The same arms, with a crescent for difference, were in a panel of stone over the entrance of the old porch. When the latter was rebuilt, this panel was placed against the interior face of its east wall."

Edward Lawrence was probably also responsible for the nave roof which replaced an earlier, lower and more shallowly pitched one, the outlines of which are still visible at the west end. The 17th century roof is of barrel vault form divided into five bays of four panels by timber ribs with quartered Lawrence and Washington shields of arms masking the four intersections at the centre. Internal redecoration may have followed this work as a fragment of 17th century stencilled floral pattern still remains above the north lancet window in the nave. The nave roof was extensively repaired in 1954.

The former bell frame, destroyed by death watch beetle and removed in 1954, was of 17th century date and perhaps contemporary with the 2nd and 3rd bells cast in 1634 by Anthony Bond – an itinerant bell-founder having no known connection with the local family of the same name.

The 18th century

A plain oak table in the vestry with square legs and a moulded stretcher is of 18th century date, and the west window was probably renewed or inserted in the 17th or 18th century. It appears to have been a somewhat unsuccessful attempt to reproduce a mediaeval design in a semi-classical idiom, being of three trefoiled lights with vertical tracery in a four centre head, but with wide flat mullions and tracery bars, and having a projecting surround and sill in the form of a classical architrave.

The 19th century

Although there are no faculty records, the chancel and south porch were rebuilt at the expense of the Rev. Nathaniel Bond, rector 1852-89, at some time between 1852 and 1861, as Hutchins' editors (3rd edition: 1861) say: "The chancel and porch have lately been rebuilt by the Rev. Nathaniel Bond, the present rector, who has also placed a new ornamental roof on the north aisle."

The east window is of three cinquefoiled lights with vertical tracery in a pointed head, and a segmental headed doorway in the north wall has since been blocked. The roof is of exposed boarding and rafters divided into two bays by three arch braced collar trusses supported on stone corbels, those in the four corners being carved with foliage, whilst the centre two feature painted Bond shields of arms with foliage carved sides. The north transept roof is of plaster between exposed rafters and divided into two bays by three arch braced collar trusses with wall posts rising from shaped and moulded stone corbels. The roof of the south chapel, probably of an earlier date, has a plain plastered ceiling with sloping soffites divided into two bays by a truss, the bottom chord of which, with arch braced feet, shows below the ceiling.

The south chapel is now used as a vestry, and in it is preserved the mechanism of a barrel organ in use in the church on a former gallery until the surprisingly late date of about 1890. It has three barrels with a gearing system,

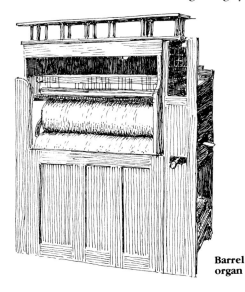

Barrel organ

and could play 24 different hymn tunes. It was made by J. W. Walker and Co. of London, and a similar but smaller instrument by the same firm at Tyneham was dated 1858. Although barrel organs were played mechanically by means of staples or projections on the barrels operating valves in a set order to produce given tunes, the notes were produced by air pumped from a bellows passing through varying sized pipes just as in a manual (i.e. keyboard operated) pipe organ. When barrel organs were replaced by manual organs, they were seldom discarded entirely, as economies could be achieved by re-using the pipes in building the new instrument, and such was the case here and at Tyneham. However, due to several exchanges of parts and organs at various times between the four churches at Steeple, Tyneham, Creech and Church Knowle, the original barrel organ parts have become separated. At Tyneham, where an American organ had been purchased in 1872, the old barrel organ was later dismantled, in 1890, when its casing was used to make the vestry cupboard at Steeple whilst the pipes were used in building the manual organ at Creech chapel. The pipes and casing of the Steeple barrel organ were used in building a manual organ here, but when Tyneham church was closed in 1943, its organ was moved to Steeple and the Steeple organ was moved to Church Knowle where the pipes and casing of the old barrel organ are consequently now to be found.

Studland
(St. Nicholas)

IN THE words of Sir Stephen Glynne, who visited Studland church in 1842: "This delightful village, situated on the border of Poole Harbour, and embosomed in wood, is no less remarkable for its interesting little Norman church than for the beauty of its scenery... The churchyard is beautifully planted, and surrounded by cypress; myrtles and roses grow up the walls of the church." Apart from the myrtles and roses, this description is just as applicable today, and the church has the distinction of being one of only a dozen or so complete or near complete Norman village churches in England. Moreover the Norman work is built around the core of a still earlier pre-conquest structure, so that it can be regarded as the oldest surviving complete church in Dorset.

In view of its Saxon origin and the quality and extent of the subsequent Norman work, it was evidently a church of some importance during the 11th and 12th centuries, and was in all probability a minster church serving an area covering the eastern part of Purbeck approximating to the domesday hundred of Aylswood. In most other cases villages or towns associated with minster churches have grown considerably, accompanied by a comparable growth in the church itself, but Studland has retained its small village character over the centuries, so that its ancient church has survived practically in its original state.

Much of what is known of the construction of the building, particularly concerning the underlying pre-conquest portions, results from an extensive investigation and programme of preservation (rather than restoration) works undertaken in 1881 under the direction of G. R. Crickmay. The builder, William Masters Hardy of Swanage, kept detailed records of the methods employed

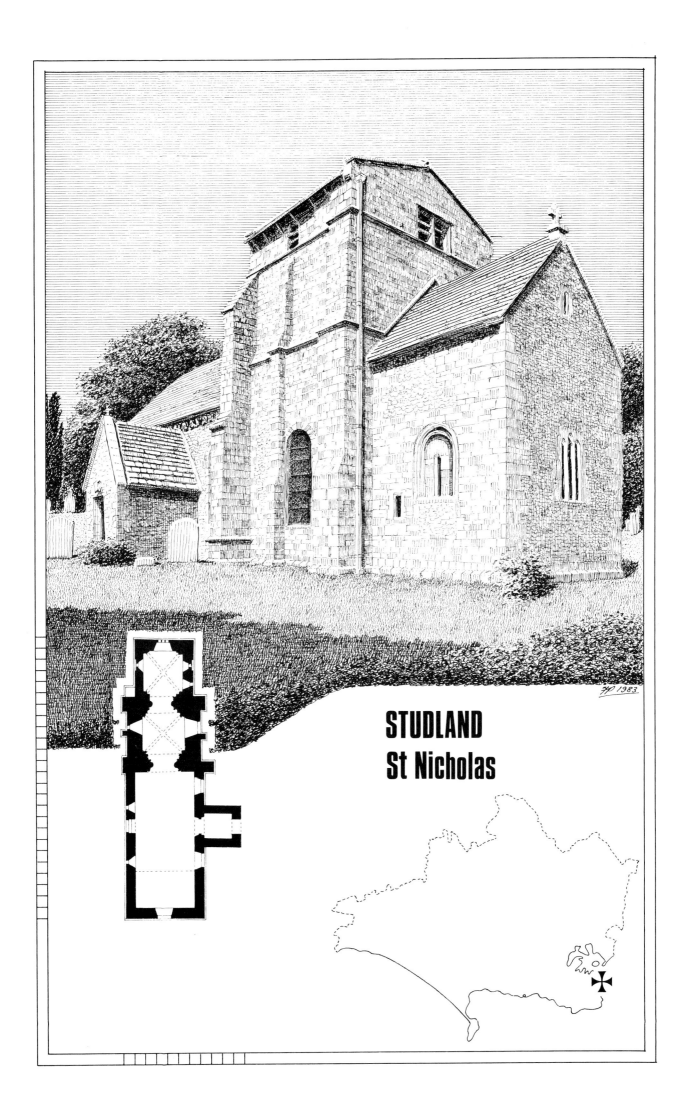

STUDLAND
St Nicholas

and of the interesting discoveries which came to light, and later wrote a comprehensive article on the subject which was published in DNHAS Proceedings Vol. 12, pp164-179. Subsequent quotations are from that article unless otherwise stated.

The 11th century

The original church was probably built shortly before the the Norman Conquest, and was of precisely the same axial plan form of chancel-tower-nave as at present, except that the nave was apparently on a slightly different alignment. No original walling remains visible internally due to the subsequent 12th century facing, but much of the original rubble walling remains visible externally, notably in the east wall of the chancel which remains virtually complete, and in the north and south walls of the chancel and tower where much of the original rubble work remains between the later Norman ashlar facing. The original pre-conquest tower, perhaps not a true tower as such, evidently only extended as far as the top of the present second stage as there are said to be no signs of earlier rubble work in the upper part.

Towards the end of the 11th century the nave was rebuilt to the same size as before, but evidently on a different alignment, as earlier foundations were exposed in 1881:

"An interesting example of the 'The Twist' was revealed during the excavations. The old foundation appeared eighteen inches out from the plinth at the N.W. corner, diminishing to nothing at the chancel, while on the S. side the plinth-line was the same distance the other side of the foundation line, the error tapering to nothing at the middle buttresses of the tower. Further investigation showed that inside on the north foundation and outside of the south a fresh line of foundation had been laid down."

The late 11th century nave walls survive basically intact, except for later corbel tables and the 18th century windows, and include a small round headed window in the west part of the north wall, the head of another in the

11th century window

south wall opposite, and opposing north and south doorways. The plainer north doorway is spanned by a keyed lintel below a semi-circular relieving arch, whilst the south doorway has a keyed lintel forming part of a plain ashlar recessed tympanum within a semi-circular unmoulded outer arch springing from jamb shafts with scalloped capitals and chamfered abaci.

Most of the walls were underpinned in 1881 when several stones re-used from an earlier building were observed in the old foundation walling: "In the old foundations were bedded massive stone steps, rudely axed, with morticed holes, about four inches square, to admit the door jambs... evidently remains from some very ancient villa, Saxon holding, or strong keep, worked out of local sandstone and of the consistence of the hoary and lonely Agglestone Rock on the heath. Also a huge keystone of an arch, suitable for a radius of five feet, was

South doorway

turned up; likewise a handmill formed by two round stones about eighteen inches in diameter, one of them having a hole at its centre."

The severe cracking which must have occurred before the completion of the 12th century work, and which is still to be clearly seen, was due to the original church having been built on ground which varied in bearing capacity between one side of the building and the other, giving rise to considerable differential settlement:

"The early builders found that one part of the ground consisted of soft red sand, so soft that no pickaxe was needed to remove it, and another section of hard sand and ironstone. To obviate building on such an unequal basis they threw in a layer of strong pipe-clay about three feet thick and five wide, which appears to have been well consolidated... and, as it happened, the clay about four feet from the floor line became soft and the worms made the clay a favourite haunt, and burrowed it through and through, softening and weakening the whole foundation, threatening the final collapse of the fabric.

"Upon this clay the foundations, formed of very rough sandstone filled in with sand and earth without mortar of any kind, were put in up to the ground line. "Ecclesiastical customs further aided to endanger the church: eg., the endeavour of the monks to bury their dead near to the Holy Place causing them to dig the vaults and graves close to the foundations, some sepulchres were deeper than the original substructure, particularly on the south side; and it appeared evident also that the Saxon builders did not foresee that their Norman successors would raise a weighty superstructure on the weak basis of their workmanship."

As was usually the case the mortar used in the earlier work was of a weak consistency:

"That of the earliest portion of the building – namely, the core between the walls, the rough-footing, and rubble-work – had little lime in it, and the loamy sand and fine grit had been taken from the churchyard, and in colour was umber. The mortar of the ashlar work, piers, and arches, which may be classed as Norman work, was whiter and of better substance chiefly consisting of lime and grit in equal quantities like that in the work of Corfe Castle; while both work and mortar of the S.W. buttress, which may be assigned to the 14th century, was the best, the mortar being as hard as cement."

The 12th century

The Norman work was essentially what would these days be termed a refurbishment or face-lift operation, designed to enhance the appearance of the building rather than to increase its size. The characteristically high Saxon proportions still apparent externally were modified internally by the provision of groined vaulting to the chancel and lower storey of the tower in association with new wall facing and casing of the arches with typical Norman mouldings. New windows were inserted, and externally, corbel tables were added to the eaves whilst plinths, buttresses and ashlar facings were grafted on to the older rubble walls:

"Many indications were discovered that all the faced stone inside and out, even the plinths and thin stone foundation which bears it, were additions to an earlier building of rubble-work. The band of ashlar-work each side of the chancel was a thin face of stone with no bond into the wall... The north wall of the chancel reveals how the Norman insertions were made. For five or six feet from the foundation there is the rough early rubble-work. Then can be seen a belt of ashlar, into which a pure Norman window has been inserted. The coating of ashlar from six to nine inches on the bed is inside and out, but the core of the wall (found while fixing the iron binding rods) is of rubble, and this rubble continues above the ashlar until the roof is reached, while the Norman work is notched into the ancient quoins at the angle, and so straight-faced as to leave the older wall crooked."

In most Dorset churches where any Norman work survives, it is usually in the form of isolated features, but here at Studland all the characteristic Norman elements are present in one building, comprising corbel tables, windows, doorways, arches and vaulting. The interior in particular, dominated by the semi-circular arches and vaulting at the east end, retains its impressive and unchanged Norman character. The arches are semi-circular and of two orders, the inner roll moulded on the

Norman capitals of east arch

underside and the outer roll moulded on the west facing angles, all springing from rounded respond shafts having variously carved scalloped capitals. The abacus of the central shaft on the north side of the eastern arch is rounded and flanked by square abaci enriched with chevron ornament, but all the remainder are square and plain. The vaulting is of the simplest quadripartite form having intersecting diagonal roll moulded ribs which spring from vaulting shafts in the angles with cushion capitals.

Norman capitals of west arch

"The groins are of Purbeck 'burr' and soft enough to be carved with a knife, wondrously light for such architecture, being porous; the 'burr' is unfitted for facing. The stone can be obtained only from rocks which appear at low tide thirty yards E. of the stone quay at Swanage. There are no other arches in the neighbourhood turned with this stone. A proper radiation has been maintained of the stones in the arches."

On the east side of the chancel arch the upper parts of the responds and the adjacent vaulting shafts have been subsequently cut away, presumably to house the ends of a later mediaeval rood gallery, as there are corbels which would have supported the rood beam itself on the west side of the same arch.

Corbel table

Externally, the most striking features are the corbel tables under the eaves on either side of the nave, each corbel having characteristically vigorous Norman carvings of human and animal heads, mostly of grotesque form, and other devices. Originally there were similar corbel tables to the eaves on both sides of the chancel, and these appear to have survived until well into the 19th century, as Sir Stephen Glynne who visited the church in 1842 recorded: "Beneath the roof of both nave and chancel, externally, runs a cornice composed of pure Norman ornaments; representing heads, grotesque animals, & c."

It was found in 1881 that some of these corbels had been re-used back to front at some time previously in effecting repairs to ashlar work:

"Some of the stones of the ancient eaves-course were (removed from their original place), and were worked into the south wall as ashlar on some occasion when the roof was being repaired. The moulded corbels on each side of the gable remain in their original position, and formed part of this course, which once ran the entire length of the eaves on either side of the chancel. Three or four of the stones can easily be seen below the eaves on the south."

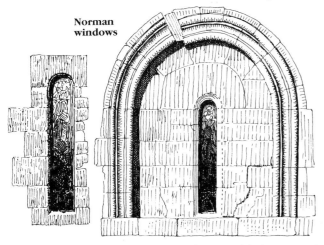

The interior which still retains much of its Norman character and atmosphere

[Photograph: Colin Graham]

The tower, having been largely refaced in ashlar incorporating shallow pilaster-like buttresses, it was evidently intended to add a further full stage on the top. Work to this upper stage, including the lower parts of the belfry windows with jamb shafting, had progressed some way when no doubt due to increasing failure of the arches beneath, the Norman builders prudently went no further, and roofed the uncompleted tower in the low gabled form in which it still remains. Of the four gable kneelers, the two at the western corners do not accord with the pitch of the roof, as if they were intended for a steeper roof, or were perhaps re-used from the original west gable of the nave.

The font is probably contemporary with the Norman work and takes the form of a plain convex sided circular bowl having a circular plinth mounted on a later square base. In 1881 it was observed: "The stone which supports the bowl is a window head, similar to the one inserted in the N.W. window, evidently taken from the N.E. nave window."

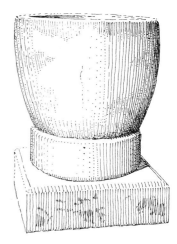

The font

The 13th – 16th centuries

Since the 12th century the church has not been enlarged at all, and as subsequent alterations have been minimal, there are remarkably few later mediaeval features. The east window of the chancel is a 13th century

Chancel, east window

A further stone from this corbel table came to light when fixing new rainwater guttering, and was salvaged and reset under the kneeler on the north east corner of the tower.

Three narrow round headed windows of this period still remain in their original positions – one at high level in the east gable of the chancel, one in the north wall of the ground stage of the tower, and one in the north wall of the chancel. This latter window is set within a larger round

Norman windows

headed recessed ashlar panel with a moulded surround, and a similar recessed panel on the south side originally contained a similar window, but it was subsequently converted into a doorway or larger window which has in its turn been replaced by the present replica window.

graduated triple lancet and is of interest in that the centre light has an early form of angular cusping. Evidently the initial differential settlement of the building, particularly in the lower part of the tower, must have been of continuing concern during the mediaeval period, for a large buttress was added at the south west corner, probably in the 14th century. This might have been associated with repairs to the tower as a whole, for in 1881 when the tower roof was closely inspected:

"The roof was found to be of rude carpentry, great

A print of 1820 by J. M. Colson showing the chancel with its 18th century half-hipped roof. The Rev. J. M. Colson was rector of Studland from 1786 until his death in 1837
[Source: Dorset County Museum collection]

By kind permission of the Dorset Natural History and Archaeological Society, Dorset County Museum, Dorchester, Dorset, as are all illustrations with a similar credit line.

timber principals, purlins, and rafters with rough oaken shingles laid across about three inches asunder covered with cast-lead ³/₁₆th inch thick without wooden rolls, and the lead in good condition. The earliest date scored thereon is 1381."

Other mediaeval items include a plain Purbeck marble coffin lid in the floor at the east end of the nave, a small stone carved with a floral device reset in the north east external angle of the chancel on the north face, a small square headed window set low in the south wall of the chancel, and a Purbeck marble table tomb against the north wall of the chancel, with cusped panels enclosing blank shields which were originally fitted with brass shields of arms.

The 17th – 18th centuries

The south porch is probably of 17th century date, and it may possibly have replaced an original 12th century porch, as part of a roll moulded arch voussoir has been built into the east wall externally. Owing to the lack of post 12th century alterations such a voussoir cannot have come from an archway in the main body of the church, and seems therefore likely to have originally formed part of the entrance archway of a Norman porch. Hutchins (1st edition: 1774) remarked: "The door of the S. porch is remarkably narrow and low, hardly five feet high." Other 17th century items include two chairs with carved seats and rails and arcaded back panels, and the first two verses of psalm 84 painted within a decorative border on the east wall of the nave.

During the 18th century four large round headed windows were inserted in the south wall of the tower and south and west walls of the nave, to admit more light into an interior which must have been somewhat dark before. They are of characteristic 18th century untraceried round headed form, and although they detract from the pure Norman aspect of the building, they have in fact a greater affinity with the old work than later mediaeval windows would have done. These windows would have been relatively recent in Hutchins' time, and he evidently approved of them: "Those on the S. and at the W. end, are enlarged, and neatly sashed, in order to give air to the church, which before was exceeding damp." He also approved of the 18th century reredos which then existed: "The altar piece is of neat wainscot, on which are the Ten Commandments, Creed and Lord's Prayer in gold letters,

done at the charge of Mr Culme, late rector." (Benjamin Culme was rector 1718-44). Such altar pieces were popular during the 18th century, but very much less so in the 19th. It still remained in 1842 when Sir Stephen Glynne visited the church, who said: "The east end of the chancel is taken up by an inappropriate Grecian altar piece." The north and south doorways are fitted with pairs of doors having fielded panels of 18th century date, and all of these items, windows, doors and altar piece probably formed part of a general refitting scheme. This may also have included the provision of a former gallery approached by way of an external flight of steps through a round headed doorway at high level in the north wall of the nave since blocked, and some re-roofing works entailing alterations to the east gable of the chancel. In old prints this gable appears as cropped or half hipped like those on the 18th century church at Horton. In 1881 it was observed:

"In a sketch by the Rev. John M. Colson, 1858, the gable is represented as 'hipped-in'. On removing the old roof it was patent by the timber that though there were no outward signs the sketch was trustworthy."

The 19th century

By 1880 the church had become in such a bad state of repair that its inherent structural weaknesses were giving rise to fears that total collapse might be imminent. In that year the recently formed Society for the Protection of Ancient Buildings were consulted and after an inspection by them it was recommended that urgent action was required in order to preserve the building. Ten or twenty years earlier the structural state of the building would have been considered hopeless and total rebuilding would have been embarked upon without a second thought. As it was the SPAB's sound advice was followed and the building was preserved in its ancient form by means of well considered and unobtrusive strengthening of the old fabric. As referred to before the architect was G. R. Crickmay, and the builder W. M. Hardy of Swanage, whose detailed notes on the work were published in DNHAS Proceedings Vol. 12 (1891), p 164-179. The article is of particular value, not only for its record of the form and construction of parts of the old building not normally visible, but for being a rare first hand account of 19th century building work of this type. Those parts of the article dealing with the construction of the old building have already been quoted under the appropriate headings, and the following extracts are concerned specifically with the repairs and strengthening work carried out in 1881:

"There were immense cracks in the walls and arches of the tower, rendering it far from secure. Heavy shores were, therefore set at the dangerous angles to receive the thrust of the interior arches and groinings, and a cutting, 7ft wide and from 4ft to 12ft deep, was excavated in sections at an average distance of 3ft from the walls (thus leaving space for their subsequent underpinning) and filled in with concrete. This extended from the east end of the chancel to the west end of the nave. ... The tower was thoroughly shored and encased, and the interior arches were wedged up with strong centres; then the underpinning commenced. This was found both difficult and dangerous, so that short sections of wall, from two to three feet at a time, were proceeded with, and even then, while the brickwork was being carried up, the core of the wall ran down like sand in the hour-glass, especially when, on one occasion, the volunteer artillery of Swanage, in close thick weather, were at heavy gun practice.

"The new work was set in wider than the base of the walls and piers within and without"... (this was done along the whole of the north side of the church and continued around the west and south sides of the nave) ... "Underpinning was unnecessary for the rest, but the foundations were cleared out, Portland cement concrete rammed in, and a water gutter hollowed on the surface. ...

"To preserve the chancel a brick beam, two feet by eighteen inches, was built in all round the walls just above the window arches, and in the centre of this beam a hollow was left, through which were run tie-rods an inch-and-a-half thick, and these were fastened at each angle by nuts and screws. Upright bars were placed at the angles. A couple of sets of bars connected, one running round the imposts of the arches and the other six feet higher, were worked into the tower.

"Although no hammering was allowed the insertion of these bars was a ticklish task, but happily no accident happened. About half-way up the tower, at the N.E. angle, the ashlar had to be removed three feet in height by twenty inches broad. There the core commenced running until no less than eight feet above the hole was entirely emptied out.

"The whole of the plaster on the interior walls was picked off. Then the difficulty had to be met how should the chancel arches be kept up? For the cracks had been filled up with old wooden wedges and plastered over. These having decayed, and the walls being a mass of small flints, chalk, and loamy sand (for there was nothing solid), the core came rattling down like dust directly the plaster was disturbed through the cracks in the groining where the wedges had been fixed. The difficulty of the running core was overcome by removing loose stones directly the running ceased, washing out the cracks, filling them with Portland cement-grout, and treating the outside face with red sandstone. Underneath the whitewash fresco paintings of figures were found on the lower parts of the groined arches and on the walls round. Traces of these frescoes are now visible. The diagonal ribs were discovered ornamented with red and blue lines."

An earlier 19th century buttress on the south side seems to have been doing more harm than good:

"A curious instance of reverence interfering with security came to light on this side. About 1840 a buttress was built at the S.E. angle, thirteen feet high and two feet six inches by two feet, battering slightly on the S. front, solid, notched into the ashlar, and tied in the angle with irons. As the buttress was dragging down the wall orders were given by Mr Crickmay for removal. Lo! three feet under the plinth a leaden coffin, a stone three feet square across it, upon which the buttress had been erected! The coffin had given in three inches. This buttress has not been replaced.

"The floor (from the choir to the chancel) has been restored to its original lines. It was level with the top of the bases of the columns. The ancient bases and the skirting-courses were discovered during the excavation. The tombstones have been relaid, as near as possible, in their former positions."

And so this remarkable and interesting building was saved for posterity, and now over 100 years later the repair and reinforcing works of 1881 are still proving effective. Subsequent works have included recasting and rehanging the bells covered by a faculty dated 11 February 1898. It was intended to strengthen the bell frame, take down the four bells, three of which were cracked and the other "almost useless from age ... and re-cast the same with the present inscriptions and date of recasting, and provide an apparatus for chiming, and rehang the same." The estimated cost was £98. One of the bells was, and still is, dated 1065 and inscribed 'Draw nigh to God'. This is an impossibly early date for a bell of this type particularly in view of the Arabic numerals and English inscription. At the time of its original casting the centre two digits were probably misplaced in the mould and it should have read '1605'.

A faculty dated 23 October 1930 was for reconstructing the nave roof at an estimated cost of £1316, the architect being Herbert H. Kendall FRIBA of Poole. The roof is of exposed trussed rafters to a high segmental profile with plastered soffites between, and divided into five bays by four square section tie beams.

Swanage
(All Saints)

THERE COULD not be a greater contrast between Studland church of the 11th and 12th centuries and this one of the 20th, but there is perhaps a tenuous link insofar as the successors of the gunners whose heavy gun practice in 1881 caused the underpinning at Studland to be so hazardous, were indirectly responsible for the origin of Swanage All Saints. For the story of this church began during the First World War when troops of the Royal Artillery were in camp at Ulwell. A wooden hut was provided for them in Washpond Lane, off Ulwell Road, for use as a recreation centre and for church services on Sundays. It was opened on 14 February 1915, and presumably on account of this date was known as the 'St Valentine's Room'. After the war the hut was re-erected on a new site in Cliff Avenue where it was enlarged by the addition of a chancel and sanctuary. In 1945 the Association of Friends of All Saints was formed with a view to raising sufficient funds to build a permanent church in this part of the town, and the efforts of the Association and the parishioners were rewarded by the building of the present church in 1956-57. The old building in Cliff Avenue was then given up, the last service there being on 4 September 1957.

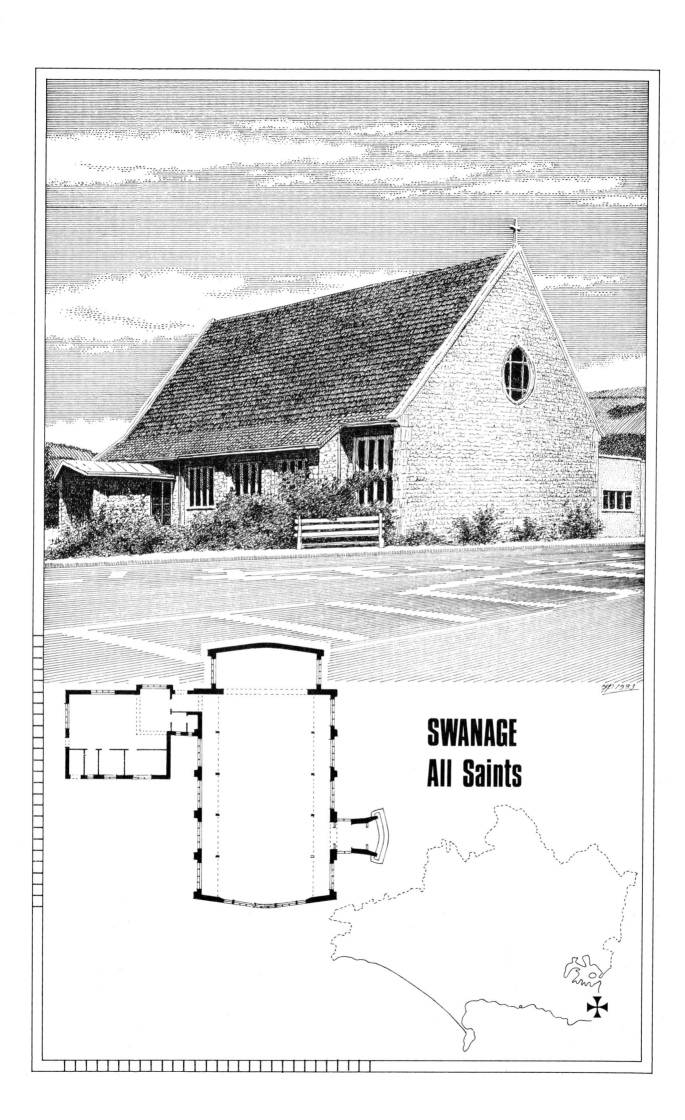

SWANAGE
All Saints

The architects for the new church were Messrs Potter and Hare of Salisbury (the practice is now known as Robert J. Potter and Partners), the builder was George Parsons of Swanage, and the basic building cost was £16,200. Fees and other expenses in connection with the building work, and furnishings, etc., brought the total cost to just over £19,000. The foundation stone is inscribed: "THIS STONE WAS LAID BY THE LORD BISHOP OF SHERBORNE 1st MARCH 1956", and the completed building was consecrated on 8 August 1957. A stone set in the east wall of the sanctuary internally came from Salisbury Cathedral, emphasising the diocesan link, and is carved with a consecration cross having the digits of the date 1957 arranged in the four arms of the cross.

The church was well designed and soundly built, and after more than 25 years still retains much of its original freshness and impact, particularly internally. It is planned on a basic rectangle with convex east and west gable walls, divided into a total of six structural bays, the eastern sanctuary bay being narrower and resulting in a greater eaves height under the continuous planes of the double pitched roof. This is covered by bold pantiles and has widely sprocketed eaves. The shaped gable walls are of random Purbeck stonework and the side walls are mostly finished in cement render, but punctuated by Purbeck stone piers which express the structural bays. The windows are straightforward rectangular ones with stout frames and mullions, of stone in the sanctuary and of wood elsewhere, divided into square and rectangular leaded panes of mostly clear glass but with random isolated obscured glass panes. There is a vertically set vesica shaped window at high level in the east gable.

Internally the wide span of the roof is broken by rows of reinforced concrete columns, in hammered or sand-blasted finish with smooth sunken arrisses, which taper towards the bottom, forming narrow aisles. The ceilings of the aisles are of shallow segmental barrel form finished in a textured render, and a very spacious effect is achieved in the nave where the parabolic ceiling, finished in shaped square fibreboard tiles, makes the maximum use of the available height under the highest part of the roof. The similarly shaped sanctuary ceiling is slightly higher and has sloping soffites at the sides. Internal finishes are mostly modern materials. The floors of the sanctuary and east bay of the nave are finished in terrazzo tiles and the remainder of the nave in vinyl tiles, whilst the walls are generally plastered, but with acoustic tiles to the west wall of the nave and random Purbeck stone to the flank walls of the sanctuary.

By contrast the oak altar table and pulpit are on more traditional lines, the pulpit forming five panelled sides of an octagon with a band of leaf carving below a corniced top, whilst the altar table is of ogee headed traceried panels divided into five sections by standards in the form of miniature two stage buttresses. The font, which was given by the parishioners of Melcombe Bingham, dates from 1751 and is of an elegant classical pattern comprising a small circular bowl with bay leaf ornament around the rim, on a concave fluted stem having acanthus ornament around the top and a moulded round base on a square sub-base. It has a round cover with an 18th century pineapple finial.

The original plans provided for a future gallery to occupy the western bay of the nave, and although this has never materialised, the original vestry at the north east corner has since been taken down and replaced by a church hall. A small commemorative plaque is inscribed: "THIS HALL WAS DEDICATED BY THE LORD BISHOP OF SHERBORNE 26th NOVEMBER 1979."

All Saints: 1751 font with pineapple finial

Swanage
(St. Mark)

HUTCHINS (1st edition: 1774) describes Herston as: "an hamlet and tything, of near 50 houses, W. of Swanwich, and adjoining to it," but since then it has lost its separate identity and has become absorbed into the general westward extension of Swanage. By the second half of the 19th century the community here had grown sufficiently to warrant the building of a separate church, and after the present site in Bell Street (named after Andrew Bell, a former rector of Swanage instituted in 1801) had been given, work was started on the new church in 1869 as recorded on a foundation stone in the east wall, simply inscribed MDCCCLXIX. The architect had been initially John Hicks of Dorchester, but after his death on 12 February 1869 the practice was taken over by G. R. Crickmay of Weymouth. Thomas Hardy had been Hicks' pupil and assistant from 1856 until 1862, and was employed by him again from July 1867 until his death in 1869; as Crickmay then employed Hardy specifically to assist in continuing the church projects already begun by Hicks, it is particularly likely that Hardy had some involvement in the design and construction of this church.

It is, as it was intended to be, a very economical design in both general concept and detail, consisting of a nave and chancel contained with a simple rectangle under one continuous double pitched roof which is extended down along part of the north side to embrace a small north aisle containing an organ bay and vestry. There is also a small separately roofed porch on the south side. The walls are faced with squared rock-faced Purbeck stone with ashlar dressings, and the roofs are covered with Purbeck stone tiles. The details are equally simple and economical, all the windows being in the form of lancets, mostly in pairs, but arranged as a graduated triplet in the east wall and as a graduated quintuplet in the west wall. The heads of the lights are trefoiled in the chancel, but plain elsewhere. A bell cote is situated on the ridge of the roof and supported by the wall beneath dividing the nave from the chancel.

Internally the chancel arch is pointed of two continuous chamfered orders, and the north arcade arches are similar. The nave roof is a typical Hicks design of plastered soffites between exposed rafters divided into four main bays by arch braced scissors trusses with wall posts rising from stone corbels carved with prism

**SWANAGE
St Mark**

ornament. The profiles of the trusses exactly fit the chancel arch, and each main bay is sub-divided by a secondary truss of similar design, but without arch bracing, wall posts and corbels.

The 17th century font was formerly in St Mary's church, and its hexagonal Purbeck stone bowl is ornamented by pairs of round headed panels in 12th century fashion, the two panels on the east face being coupled and inscribed C ED CW IC 1663 Y. The adjacent panel is inscribed LC BAP 16TH APRL.

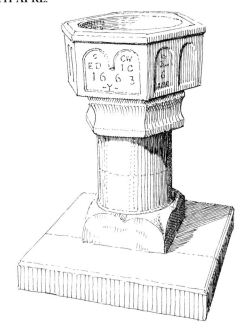

The font

Although the church was begun in 1869, work remained at a standstill for some time after being roofed in due to a shortage of funds, but it was later resumed and the completed church was consecrated on 25 April 1872. The Dorset County Chronicle reported on the building and the consecration service in its issue of 2 May 1872 from which the following extracts are taken:

"On Thursday last, when the new church at Herston, dedicated to the Evangelist whose memory the Church of England that day commemorated, was consecrated by the Right Rev. Dr Moberly, the lord Bishop of the Diocese... For some considerable period Sunday evening service was held in the modest little schoolroom at Herston, which was erected some years ago. A strong feeling as to the necessity of an additional place of worship was gradually developed... An elevated and conspicuous plot of ground, 90 feet square, the munificent gift of Mrs Serrel of Durnford Hall, Langton Matravers, was enclosed as the site, and that benevolent lady likewise contributed the handsome sum of £200 ... in 1869 the foundation-stone was laid, a record of the ceremony being afterwards inscribed on a stone which may now be seen externally underneath the east window. The whole of the work has cost only £1,400, therefore the expectation that there would be no delay caused from any lack of funds was reasonable enough. But when the outer portion of the structure had been raised – about £900 expense having been incurred – operations were after all suspended, for it was judiciously determined to adhere to the resolution not to run into debt. Contrary to expectation the work was thus for some time at a standstill, but about last October it was resumed, and ever since then the building has progressed slowly but steadily.

"The building may be described as a plain Early English village church, inexpensive, but, nevertheless pretty and of effective design. The plans were originally prepared by the late Mr Hicks of Dorchester, the work having been carried out under the personal supervision and direction of Mr G. R. Crickmay, the well-known architect of Weymouth... The masonry etc, has been executed in a very satisfactory manner by native workmen under Mr Felix G. Fooks, of Herston, Mr Linnington, of Swanage, having superintended the plastering."

In more recent years, in about 1975, the church was enlarged by the addition of new vestries and ancillary rooms at the south west corner and linked to the old porch. It is flat roofed, and although the east wall, incorporating the old window from the west wall of the porch, is faced in matching rock-faced Purbeck stone, the remaining walls are faced in grey sand-faced brickwork.

Swanage
(St Mary)

DURING THE middle ages Swanage was no more than a small village, probably clustered around the still existing mill pond and St Mary's church which itself enjoyed only the status of a chapel to the more important church at Worth Matravers. In those days the vicar of Worth or his curate would have regularly made the journey between the two places, and the track which they took across the downs is still known as Priest's Way. However, Swanage must have grown in size or importance during the latter half of the 15th century for it became a separate parish in about 1506, although it still remained essentially a fishing village and stone quarrying centre until the 19th century when the growing popularity of its equable climate and seaside situation brought about a rapid change in both character and size into the popular resort it is today. This pattern of growth is reflected in the parish church where the tower is all that is left of the mediaeval building, the rest having disappeared in the course of rebuilding and considerable enlargements in 1859-60 and 1907-08.

Although most of the old building was taken down in 1859, a considerable amount is known concerning it from the faculty plan which shows the form and extent of the former building, old prints of the exterior, and pre-1859 descriptions. Hutchins (1st edition: 1774) described the old church thus:

"It is a large ancient building, and consists of a chancel, body, a narrow N. isle, almost equal with the chancel, a small S. isle, a pretty high tower, in which are four bells and a clock. The body is covered with lead, the rest with tile. The chancel is large, and is one-third the length of the whole fabric. The N. isle belongs to Godlingston farm; the S. to no particular place or person. On the E. is a pedestal for an image; on the S. a nich for holy water. Near it an arch in the wall, and under it a narrow tomb of grey Purbeck marble, but without inscription. The church seems to have been built at different times as the inhabitants increased, and it became a parochial church, being formerly but a chapel to Worth. Perhaps the present body was the ancient chapel."

SWANAGE
St Mary

The editors of the 2nd edition of 1796 supplement this description with a contributed section by Thomas Manville, who, besides propounding a rather fanciful theory as to the extreme age of the tower, gives some useful additional information:

"From the foundation of a wall two feet and a half thick, lately discovered by digging a grave in it, it appears to have been only the same width of the tower originally, but has since been enlarged by removing the North wall farther from the centre. Its length remains the same as at first. That this edifice is of a much later date than the tower is evident from its having no wall on the west, except the segment that was built when it was widened, as before mentioned; the East wall of the tower serving for this purpose. On the top of the chancel is a stone cross. The site of this church being very low ground, renders it damp and unwholesome in wet weather."

Sir Stephen Glynne visited the church in 1830 and his architecturally knowledgeable account is of particular value:

"The church is plain and of singular appearance, but a great part appears to be of late date, perhaps as late as the time of Elizabeth. It consists of a lofty nave and chancel, and a south transept. The chancel has a north aisle. At the west end is a lofty and a curious tower, which appears to be of very early character, plain and rude. It has four distinct stages tapering towards the summit, and without buttresses; the top entirely plain. The lowest stage has a plain pointed doorway; the two next have plain single openings; and the belfry story a window of two lights. The arch from the tower to the nave is pointed and low. To this tower a very early date has been assigned, but on no fixed data. The roof of the church is tiled, and the nave and chancel thrown into one space of great height. The body has evidently been altered at different times. The northern windows are square and of two lights set high in the wall. Those on the south of the nave are in two heights, and appear to be of the time of James I. The chancel has square-headed windows on the south; and at the east end a large one with square head, four lights and transom the interior face having a contracted arch with pierced trefoils in the spandrels. In the north aisle of the chancel is a plain lancet at the east end, and a double one on the side. There is no regular division between the chancel and its aisle, which however extends much beyond the nave. The font is octagonal and Norman — each face moulded with plain Norman arches, placed on a circular pedestal. In the south transept is a monumental arch. The interior is neatly arranged, but considerably modernised. There is in the west gallery an organ that can be played either by the hand, or with keys."

All these accounts tally well with the faculty plan which shows the pre-1859 church to have consisted of the still remaining west tower, a nave, south transept and south porch in the same positions and of the same sizes as their present counterparts, but with a narrower chancel having a projecting chapel on the north side. Although there must have been an archway of some sort between the south transept and nave, all the other internal structural divisions had at some time been removed, so that the nave, chancel and north chapel formed one large space under a common double pitched roof. Two pre-1859 prints of the exterior, one from the south east and one from the north east, show that the ridge of this roof was centred over the nave, with differing eaves heights to accommodate the varying wall alignments on the north side, and resulting in a curiously irregular east gable to the chancel. This unconventional effect was heightened by an equally unconventional east window of four lights with glazed spandrels under a transome with a row of superimposed tracery lights above, all under a square label. Parts of this window were re-used to form the present south west window of the nave which is of a similar pattern, but of three lights.

On the old plan it is noticeable that the south walls of the nave and chancel are in direct alignment with the south wall of the tower (as they still remain in the present building), and that the short section of north wall of the chancel similarly lined with the north wall of the tower. This fact, combined with Thomas Manville's account of finding the foundations of an earlier north wall of the nave in line with the north wall of the tower, makes it quite clear that originally the tower, nave and chancel were all of the same width, when the former recess on the north side of the chancel can be seen to have taken a conventional chapel or aisle-like form.

The 13th century

Evidently some 13th century work still remained in the church before the rebuilding of 1859-60 as Sir Stephen Glynne referred to lancet windows in the north chapel, which also appear on one of the old prints referred to. In addition there are ten fragments of 13th century shafts still preserved loose in the present church which may have originally formed parts of the chancel arch or of an arcade between the chancel and north chapel.

The 14th century

The straight joint externally in the masonry between the tower and nave on the south side, still evident in the present building, seems always to have been a feature at this point according to Thomas Manville's observation which he rightly construed as a junction between work of differing periods. However, in the 18th and early 19th centuries when mediaeval architecture was not well understood, very plain work was usually equated either with secular use or great age, and the tower was assumed on that account to have been considerably older than the body of the church. The lower three stages are now considered to be of 14th century date, and the straight joint is consistent with a tower of this period having been added to the earlier, 13th century nave.

The upper stage was added during the 17th century, but the lower three stages are original and unusually plain for 14th century work, without buttresses or other embellishments, the division between the diminishing stages being marked by plain weathered offsets. All the windows of this period are in the form of small rectangular loop lights, arranged in two tiers in the north, south and west faces of the second stage, and one in each of the four faces of the third stage (two now covered by clock faces), these latter four being the original belfry windows. The original west doorway, with continuously chamfered jambs and pointed head, has since been partially blocked and filled with a 15th century window, and the original tower arch has also been blocked.

The upper half of a coffin lid with a decorative cross head and a complete coffin lid with a foliated cross on a

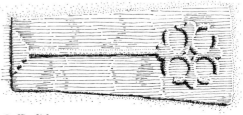

Coffin lid

SWANAGE St Mary   development

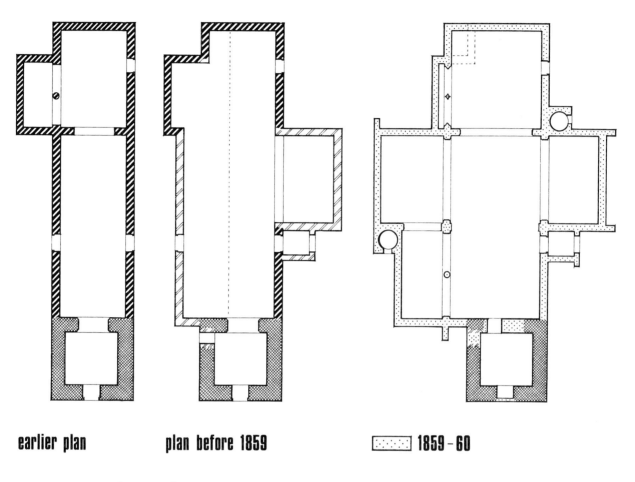

earlier plan   plan before 1859   ▦ 1859-60

▨ 13th cent (probably)

▬ 14th cent

▨ 17th cent (probably)

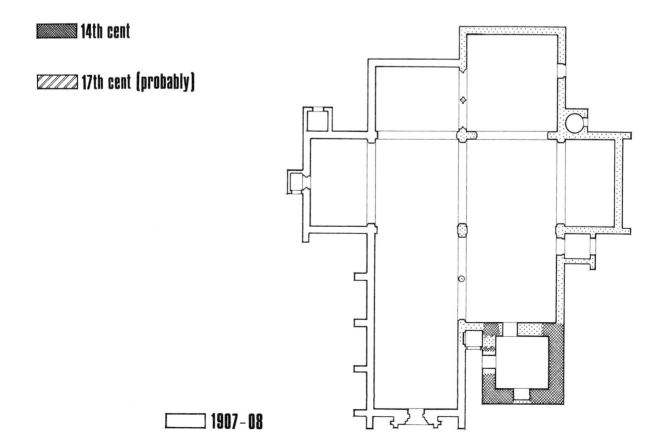

□ 1907-08

stepped calvary now reset against the north side of the north arcade pier are both of early 14th century date. The former four light east window of the chancel already referred to was of late 14th or early 15th century date, and the present south west window of the nave, of three trefoiled lights with six vertical traceried lights above a transome under a square head, is of similar design incorporating parts of the original east window together

Nave,
south-
west
window

with the wholly original rear arch which has quatrefoil pierced spandrels. According to Sir Stephen Glynne's account and the old prints of the exterior, there were a number of square headed windows in the old building, and when members of the DNHAS visited the church on 9 September 1896 (Proceedings Vol. 18, p xlv – xlvii) the Rev. T. A. Gurney referred to three old windows re-used in the present building: "the Perpendicular window now on the south side of the nave, which used to stand at the east end of the Perpendicular church, as the picture shows and the two windows in the south transept which used to be south chancel windows." These latter two windows in the south wall, each of two trefoiled lights with vertical tracery in a square head are therefore presumably also basically of late 14th or early 15th century date, but they have been considerably restored.

The 15th century

The present west window, fitted into the original door opening, is of two cinquefoiled lights with vertical tracery

Tower,
west
window

in a pointed head, of typical 15th century form, but with unusually wide lights as if made specifically to fit this opening. On the other hand this conflicts with Sir Stephen Glynne's account which infers that this opening was still a west door in 1830, so presumably the window was formerly in some other part of the church.

The church possesses a fine mid 15th century brass, now reset in the tower vestry, depicting William Clavell and his first and second wives Margaret and Alice with a black letter inscription, and there are four other brasses of later dates. These record John Harve (1510), Henry Welles and his first wife Mary (1607 and 1560), Thomas Serrell (1639) and Susan Cockram (1641).

The 17th century

Sir Stephen Glynne considered parts of the old church to have been of the time of Queen Elizabeth 1 (1558-1603), and that transomed windows on the south side of the nave were of the reign of James 1 (1603-1625). These latter dates would certainly tally with the upper stage of the tower, the addition of which is likely to have been associated with other works in the church itself. It was probably at this time that the nave was widened, and as this would have necessitated an entirely new roof, it seems that the chancel and its north chapel also were included under the same wide span roof to result in the irregular gable arrangement at the east end visible in old prints. Such a roof would have in its turn permitted the removal of the chancel arch and other internal structural divisions to open up the interior into basically one large space in line with 17th century patterns of worship. Taking Hutchins' and Sir Stephen Glynne's accounts together there would appear to have been a table tomb monument, an image bracket and a piscina in the south transept, all indicative of a mediaeval origin, but it was probably largely rebuilt or remodelled in association with other 17th century work. It was of two storeys, the upper part forming a gallery lit by a tall window in the south gable and a dormer arrangement on the east side. The added upper stage of the tower followed the simple character of the older part, with a weathered offset, plain parapet, and belfry windows each of a pair of plain pointed lights filled with stone louvres. The font, now in St Mark's church at Herston, is dated 1663, and a stone now reset in the north aisle, inscribed with the names of the churchwardens and dated 1684, may have recorded the completion of some phase of 17th century work.

The 18th century

Two faculties of 1792 and 1793 were for rebuilding the galleries, appropriating pews and repairs to the walls, and the resultant work is referred to by Hutchins' editors (2nd edition: 1796): "This ancient church has lately undergone some considerable repairs. It has been entirely new seated and cieled, and spacious and handsome galleries have been built for the better accommodation of the inhabitants; the expence of which amounted to about £400."

The 19th century

The faculty for rebuilding and enlargement is dated 17 March 1859, the architect was T. H. Wyatt, and the estimated cost £2160. Work must have started soon after this date for the Dorset County Chronicle reported in its issue of 30 June 1859: "The ceremony of laying the foundation stone of the new church took place on Wednesday the 15th inst. The whole church is to be rebuilt, excepting the tower, and the style will be perpendicular Gothic architecture... Such parts of the old

Two views of the old church drawn by the Rev. J. M. Colson (died 1837), and printed by 'Cowell's Anastatic Press, Ipswich'. Together they give an accurate picture of the church's form before the rebuilding of 1859-60

[Source: Dorset County Museum collection]

Another print of the old church engraved from a drawing by W. A. Miles of 1826

[Source: Dorset County Museum collection]

windows as are sufficiently good will be re-used and adapted... The expense is estimated at £2180. It is to be roofed in before the winter, and to be completed by about May next. The diocesan architect, T. H. Wyatt, Esq., has supplied the plans, and Mr Mondey, of Dorchester, is the builder."

The anticipated completion in May was not achieved, and inevitably the estimated cost was exceeded, but the consecration service was reported in the Dorset County Chronicle of 26 July 1860.

"On Thursday last the newly-erected edifice – for so we may term it, nearly the whole having been rebuilt, with the exception of the tower – was consecrated by the Lord Bishop of the diocese... There are likewise galleries for the children in the transepts, which are so exceedingly light that they detract nothing from the beauty of the general arrangements, and thus extra accommodation is obtained which could not otherwise be had, owing to the difficulties connected with the site... close to the entrance is a fine Purbeck marble font, with an old Norman column, to which have been added a new base and bowl... The total sum now received for the restorations, including the amount received on Thursday, is about £2,700, but about £300 more is still required."

The work of 1859-60 followed the old plan closely insofar as the nave, south transept and south porch were rebuilt in the same positions and to exactly the same dimensions as before, and although the south and east walls of the chancel were rebuilt in their original positions, the chancel was widened on the north side to include most of the former north chapel. The church as a whole was enlarged by the addition of an entirely new north aisle and transept, but both these parts have since been taken down and absorbed into the further enlargements of 1907-08. All the work of 1859-60 now therefore lies south of the line of arcading bounding the north sides of the nave and chancel, and includes the arcades themselves. The eastern half of the nave is in effect a crossing with large arches to the chancel, south transept and former north transept, each pointed and of two chamfered orders, the outer continuous and the inner springing from the responds. The roofs of the nave and south transept are double pitched and of similar construction having plastered soffites between exposed rafters divided into bays by arch braced high collar trusses with short bracketted hammer beams supported by

shaped stone corbels, and the crossing is formed impressively by two similar trusses, but with cusped arched bracing set diagonally and intersecting each other.

The chancel roof is of trussed rafter construction with plastered soffites above the exposed bottom chords which form a five sided polygonal profile, all divided into 3 bays by arch braced principals of a matching profile with short bracketted hammer beams off shaped stone corbels, two of which have foliage carving. An arcade on the north side, formerly forming a shallow recess representing the north end of the former chapel but now opening to the organ bay, is formed of two pointed arches of two chamfered orders supported by a central column of four clustered shafts and triple shafted responds. The east window is of five lights with trefoiled and quatrefoiled roundel tracery in a pointed head, whilst the side windows are plain lancets, the one on the south west being a pair with trefoiled rear arches supported on a Purbeck marble column.

The south transept has a stair turret in the angle against the chancel giving access to a gallery which is lit by a circular traceried window in the south gable, and the former north transept was similar, also with a gallery, and having a stair turret at the north west corner. Contrary to the County Chronicle's report in June 1859 that the church would be in the Perpendicular (15th century) style, most of it is in imitation of 13th century idioms, including the font which consists of a round convex bowl with roll moulded upper and lower edges supported by a round stem on a square moulded base.

Evidently some of the work proved not to have been so durable as might have been expected, for almost exactly 20 years later the Dorset County Chronicle of 13 May 1880 reported:

"On Ascension Day full evening service was held at Herston Chapel of Ease in consequence of the parish church undergoing repairs. The floor is nearly finished, and the roof (parts of which are rather in a bad state) is in hand."

The 20th century

In 1907-08 the building was again considerably enlarged into what virtually amounts to a double church, the new work forming on plan almost a mirror image of the earlier portion. In fact the new portion is labelled 'new nave' on the faculty plan, and the faculty document, which is dated 21 December 1906, refers to taking down the 19th century north aisle and transept: "and to construct a new Nave on an enlarged scale," together with a new north transept, new north entrance and other works which were to include raising the roof of the chancel. The architects were Clifton and Robinson of Swanage, and the estimated cost was £4000. The foundation stone at the north east corner is inscribed: TO THE GLORY OF GOD THIS STONE WAS LAID BY WINIFRED DAUGHTER OF THE REV. W. H. PARSONS RECTOR OF SWANAGE OCTR 10th 1907. CHURCHWARDENS C. C. DELAMOTTE G. W. T. DEANE. ARCHITECTS J. E. CLIFTON E. A. ROBINSON.

The north arcading and transept arch of the 1859-60 work were retained, and the new extension internally was carried out largely in imitation of the earlier work, with a similar form of roof construction and a repetition of the crossing effect using diagonal intersecting trusses. No doubt much of the earlier stonework was re-used, particularly in the north transept where the fenestration is similar to that of the south transept, probably denoting that some of the earlier windows were re-used. In the main body of the 1907-08 work however the 13th century style of the earlier work was discarded in favour of a 15th century idiom, the north wall being divided externally into strongly marked bays by deep buttresses with windows each of three cinquefoiled ogee lights and vertical tracery in a pointed head, the tracery of alternate windows incorporating a quatrefoil. There is a similar five light window in the west wall and large radial traceried circular windows in the north and east gables. The main entrance is at the west end, with a secondary entrance in the north wall of the transept, and the original gallery arrangement is repeated in the transept with a stair turret at the north east angle.

The work was begun on 12 August 1907, and in its report on the foundation stone laying ceremony on 10 October, the Dorset County Chronicle of 17 October 1907 stated that completion of the work was anticipated by the end of July of the following year. In fact it was completed about a month earlier than hoped for, the church being re-opened on 2 July 1908, and the Chronicle reported the event in the following week's issue of 9 July. The report refers to the fact that the population of Swanage had increased considerably since the church had been last enlarged in 1859-60, the shortage of accommodation being particularly acute during the summer months due to the annual influx of visitors and holidaymakers:

"On some Sundays in the month of August the church has been filled to overflowing at the ordinary service at eleven o'clock, and as many as a hundred or two hundred people have had to go away, quite unable to find room... There were for a while visions of building a new church of majestic proportions on some other site; but want of the necessary means curbed the ambitions of the people, and for the last few years the aim has been limited to enlarging the old parish church. At the Easter vestry of 1906 a committee was appointed... At their first meeting it was resolved unanimously to enlarge the church, and Messrs. Clifton and Robinson, architects and surveyors, of Swanage, were instructed to prepare plans for the purpose, so as to make the best use of the spare piece of ground on the north side of the church and to provide about 400 more sittings. Messrs. Clifton and Robinson are gentlemen of imagination and artistic faculty as well as of professional skill. They seemed to grasp the problem intuitively; and, surveying the enlarged church as one does to-day, it would be hard to conceive how the extra accommodation could, with the land at their disposal, have been provided in a more efficient manner, and with so admirable a combination of seemliness and spaciousness, taste and dignity. The plans having been finally approved and the specifications prepared tenders for the work were invited. Three tenders were received, two from well-known Swanage builders, and the third from a firm in Somerset who have done considerable work of church restoration in Dorset, especially at Dorchester. The following were the particulars of the three tenders: Mr Frank Smith, £6,375; Messrs Meyrick and Son, Glastonbury, £5,310; and Messrs. H. and J. Hardy, £4,700. This last tender, being by far the lowest, was accepted and the work was begun on August 12th, and has been carried on briskly ever since, while services have been held at the Gilbert Hall.

"The total cost of the work is estimated at about £5,500. Towards this amount the first £1,000 was contributed by the Swanage Church Lands Trustees, and the committee have collected over £1,700... Besides his donation of £100 Sir John Burt offered to give the committee a large piece of land, including the old stone-yard and a part of the Mill garden, on condition that they bought a piece to the west of the church to enlarge the entrance. The offer was accepted, and the condition attached to it was complied with at a cost of about £100.

"The architects have used the land available on the north side of the church by building alongside of the old nave, what is virtually a second nave... Three of the old stained-glass windows have been inserted in the new north transept, namely the Morton Pitt and Randall windows from the old transept and the Colson window from the north end of the old aisle. It is a feat worth noting that these windows were moved bodily, without being taken out of the stone tracery. Overhead a new gallery has been erected supported on girders, and corresponding in size and style with the old gallery in the south transept. The north wall of the chancel has been pierced, and twin decorated arches, harmonising with the arcade between the old and new naves, now communicate between the chancel and east end of the new nave. The organ has been removed from its old position on the north side of the chancel to the east end of the new nave. This work has been done, and the organ also enlarged, by Messrs. Vowels, organ builders, of Bristol...

The floor of the church has been raised six inches, and the Communion table also raised six inches and placed upon a magnificent dais of polished dark Purbeck marble...The stonework deserves special mention. Anybody inspecting it carefully can see that this church extension affords fine specimens of the Purbeck stone of the present day, and also ample proof that the working and use of this stone is as well understood as ever by the quarriers and stone-masons of Swanage and the district. The work has been executed throughout in Langton Matravers freestone, to correspond with the work in the old church...While the extension of the church reflects the highest praise on the skilful architects, the work does great credit to Messrs. H. and J. Hardy and their staff, especially their foreman, Mr Issac Edmonds, who had the carrying out of all the stonework. During the building operations an ancient consecration cross was discovered, and it has been built into the north wall of the new nave on the inside."

Tyneham
(St. Mary)

THE BEAUTIFUL Tyneham valley, so typical of the rugged Purbeck landscape, has an almost Shangri-la air about it, heightened no doubt in more recent years by having become a forbidden if not exactly lost valley. For in 1943 a large tract of land in this area was requisitioned by the War Office when the village of Tyneham was evacuated, and more than forty years later the valley still forms part of the army gunnery ranges. The old manor house and cottages are in ruins, and only the church and school remain complete. For most of the time since 1943 the church has been in a derelict state and boarded up, but the fabric has been preserved, and in recent years it has been repaired and brought into use as a local museum.

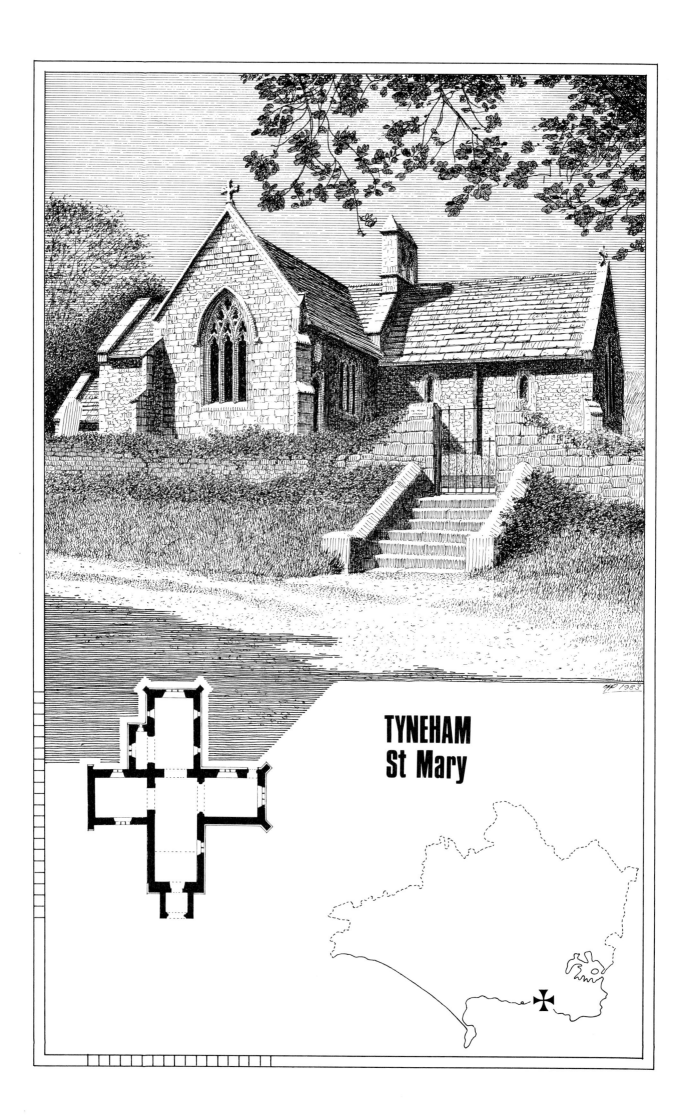

TYNEHAM
St Mary

TYNEHAM probable development

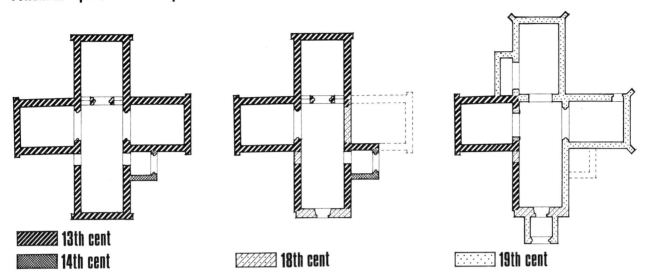

13th cent
14th cent   **18th cent**   **19th cent**

The 13th century

Although much of the building is of 19th century date, the north transept and north wall of the nave survive from the original 13th century church which must have been of cruciform plan much as at present. Surviving original features include low square set flush buttresses at the outer angles of the north transept, a double lancet window in the east wall and an unusual roughly carved piscina to the south of it in the same wall. Very probably

Double lancet window and piscina

the original building was similar in many respects to the contemporary cruciform church at nearby Church Knowle which survives basically intact from the 13th century, and the distinctive triple chancel arch there seems also to have been a feature at Tyneham, for Hutchins (1st edition: 1744) states: "There are two apertures in the side of the arch that leads into the chancel." The original south transept had already gone by Hutchins' time, having probably been taken down in 1744 when a considerable amount of repair and restoration work was undertaken.

The 14th and 15th centuries

The present west porch is constructed largely of 14th century materials, which include a segmental pointed entrance arch of two continuous chamfered orders, from a former south porch which was probably originally located in the angle between the nave and south transept, again as at Church Knowle where a 14th century porch still remains in such a position.

The double bell cote over the east gable of the nave is probably of 15th century origin, and the weathered stone top has three stoolings for some former features now gone, perhaps gable crosses, as a fragment and a more complete cross with the remnants of an inscription still remain, the latter being reset internally in the east wall of the north transept. Hutchins (1st edition: 1774) refers to a former monument of probably 15th or 16th century date: "On the N. side of the chancel, in an arch in the wall, is an old altar tomb, but no arms or inscription to direct for us for whom it was erected, nor any marks that ever there were any."

The 17th and 18th centuries

Work of the 17th century includes the square headed north doorway of the nave, since blocked, and the nearby west window of the north transept, of three square headed lights. The restoration work of 1744, referred to by Hutchins, included rebuilding the west wall of the nave and re-roofing the nave and north transept, both of which still retain plaster barrel vault ceilings of this period, that to the nave being to a somewhat irregular profile. The still remaining west gallery, with a panelled front and dentilled cornice, was probably also erected at about the same time.

Hutchins' editors (3rd edition: 1861) described the church as it was before the present south transept was added: "Though simple and somewhat picturesque, it was a mean structure, having on the south side square-headed windows with painted wooden frames." This suggests that the south wall of the nave had been rebuilt or altered during the 18th century, resulting probably from the demolition of the original 13th century south transept. A blocked segmental headed opening in the north wall of the north transept was probably a former 18th century window or doorway.

The 19th century

The original 13th century arches to the chancel and north transept were replaced by the present larger ones early in the 19th century. They are of unusual form, but nevertheless typical of the odd mixture of classical and gothic idioms which prevailed at that time, being pointed with hollow chamfered arrises springing from moulded imposts above plain jambs, and predictably Hutchins' editors (3rd edition: 1861) refer to them in derogatory terms:

"About the commencement of the present century the low arches leading to the chancel and north aisle were replaced by others of more convenient dimensions but in the bad taste which prevailed at that period. The north aisle was appurtenant to Tyneham House or Great Tyneham, by the owner of which it was exclusively occupied. It is probable, therefore, that it was originally a chantry chapel belonging to the proprietors of this estate, and there still remains a piscina in the east wall showing that an altar once occupied an adjoining spot. The body of the church having been found insufficient for the accommodation of the parishioners, the late Rev. Willam Bond, who owned this aisle, relinquished his right to it, and dedicated it to the use of the poor parishioners as free and unappropriated sittings for ever. He at the same time built a corresponding aisle or transept on the south side of the church for the exclusive use of his family and household, in lieu of the one he had relinquished. The porch, which may possibly have been as old as the 14th century, was at the same time removed to the west end, and the south wall of the nave which was much decayed was rebuilt."

The remarkably long 57 year incumbency of the Rev. William Bond lasted from his institution in 1795 until his death in 1852 at the age of 95, and the south transept added in his time probably dates from the later years of his incumbency. It opens to the nave by a pointed arch of two chamfered orders, the outer continuous and the inner springing from semi-octagonal shafts with moulded capitals, and a pointed doorway in the east wall has a stone panel above it carved with the Bond arms. The east window is of three trefoiled lights with glazed spandrels in a square head, the south window is of three trefoiled lights with cusped intersecting tracery in a pointed head, and the south window of the nave is of two trefoiled ogee headed lights with a cusped spandrel light under a square head. Internally the roof is of barrel form and divided into six bays of four boarded panels by moulded ribs with carved bosses at the intersections.

Although there appear to be no surviving faculty records, the chancel was rebuilt in 1872 according to correspondence among the Bond papers in the County Record Office (D 413). The architect was G. R. Crickmay of Weymouth, and the builder John Wellspring of Dorchester. In a letter dated 3 May 1872 Crickmay states that Wellspring is able to commence rebuilding the chancel "at once", and anticipates completion within three months, whilst a further letter dated 7 May 1872, also from Crickmay, confirms that Wellspring is ready to commence work on "Monday next". Unlike the earlier 19th century south transept the chancel is in simple 13th century style in deference to the original portion of the building, with lancet windows, the east window being a graduated triplet, and with an open timber roof of trussed rafter construction. A small compartment on the north side was presumably to accommodate an American organ purchased in 1872 (SDNQ Vol. v, p 12-15), after which the old barrel organ, inscribed "J. W. Walker, London, 1858", remained disused in the gallery until 1890 when the pipes were used in building a manual organ at Creech chapel, and the case was sold to the churchwardens at Steeple where it was converted into a vestry cupboard (see also under Steeple).

The 20th century

Re-organisation of the musical arrangements continued into this century, for the Dorset County Chronicle of 1 May 1902 reported:

"A handsome new organ has been presented to the parish church by Mr and Mrs W. H. Bond as a thank-offering for the recovery of their son, Lieut. Bond, of the Rifle Brigade, who it will be remembered received a dangerous wound while serving with his regiment during the siege of Ladysmith. An organ had been much needed for the church, and the munificence of the donors is greatly appreciated. The dedication service was of a most interesting and impressive character, and was attended by a large congregation, worshippers coming from different parts of the parishes of Steeple, Blackmanstone, Grange, Povington and Worbarrow. The service was conducted by the Rev. C. S. Homan (rector). Appropriate music was selected, Mr Mearing (Corfe Castle) ably presiding at the new organ."

Tyneham church in its post war condition with boarded up windows, in 1968
[Photograph: Rodney Legg]

Wareham
(Holy Trinity)

BRIDPORT, DORCHESTER, Shaftesbury and Wareham, being the four Dorset boroughs at the time of the domesday survey of 1086, are the oldest towns in the county, and it is significant that Shaftesbury and Wareham, both with monastic establishments within their boundaries, should have been liberally supplied with churches during the middle ages. In both cases there are said to have been as many as twelve, but at Wareham only three of the buildings survive, and only one, St Mary's, remains in use as a parish church, St Martin's and Holy Trinity having been disused as such since the 18th century. Four other Wareham churches which have now gone are known to have survived the Reformation and to have remained in use until the 17th or 18th century. All Hallows chapel was situated at the junction of Cow Lane and North Street, and St John's chapel, situated at St John's Hill where the name still survives, was in use until at least 1631. St Michael's, serving a parish in the north west quarter of the town in St Michael's Lane was still in use in 1755 when William Jennings the last rector was instituted, but it was soon afterwards converted into a barn and later demolished. St Peter's, serving a parish bounded by East Street, North Street and Dollins Lane, stood on the site of the present Corn Exchange, and not long after John Combs the last rector was instituted in 1761, it was demolished to make way for a new town hall, schoolhouse and gaol in 1768.

Holy Trinity church, although disused as such since the fire of 1762, still stands and can almost be regarded as a memorial to its last rector John Hutchins, M.A., whose famous work "The History and Antiquities of the County of Dorset", published in 1774, was written whilst rector here from 1743 until his death in 1773. It is a truly great work of painstaking research and scholarship, still indispensible to all students of any aspect of Dorset

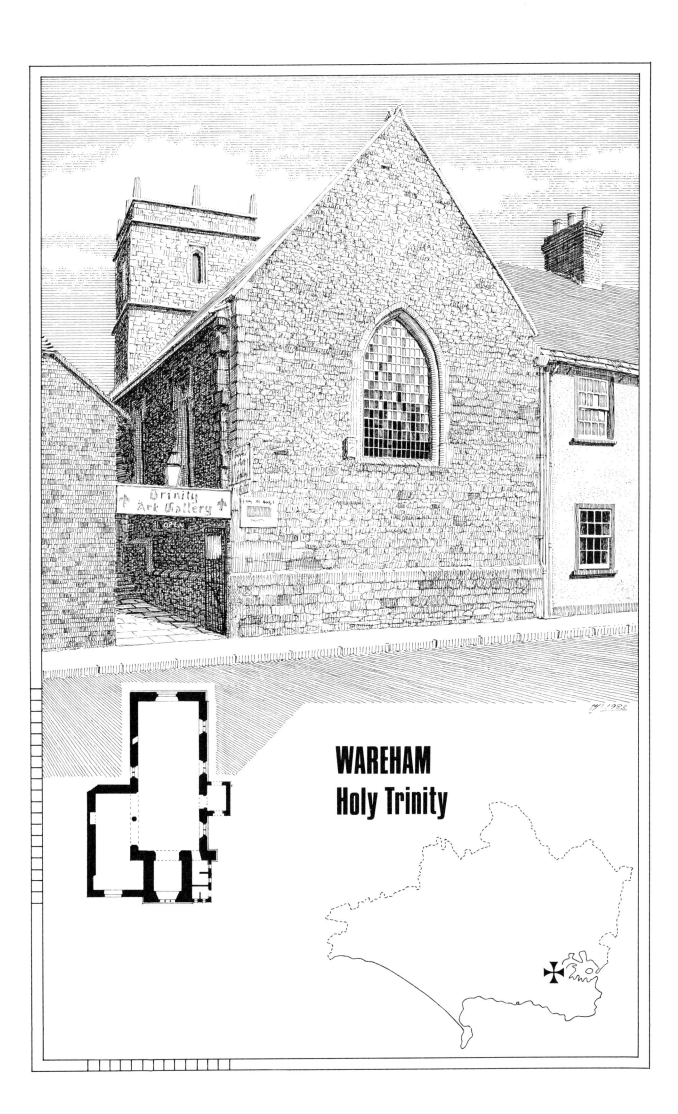

WAREHAM
Holy Trinity

history, and liberally quoted from in these pages. It is perhaps particularly appropriate to quote Hutchins' description of this church in full:

"The church of the Holy Trinity stands on the W. side of the street, near the bridge, and is small, not capable of containing all the inhabitants at once; and the hamlets in the parish must have been formerly more populous. It is very ancient, and is dedicated to the Holy Trinity, but formerly to St Andrew. For pope Eugenius III, in a bull dated 1145, reciting and confirming the possessions of Sherborne Abbey, mentions inter alia the chapel of St Andrew, in Wareham; and pope Alexander III, in a bull to the same purpose dated 1163, mentions inter alia the chapel of the Holy Trinity, omitting St Andrew's; so that it seems to have been re-dedicated in that interval; for the abbot of Sherborne was patron of this church, and of none other in the town. It consists of a chancel, a body, a small N. isle half the length of the body, at the entrance of which seems to have been a chantry. The tower is of a moderate height, adorned with battlements and pinnacles, and containing four bells. The whole of the fabric is covered in tile. It is now the mother-church of the whole town, though disused since the fire.

"Humphry Baskervil, gent. of this parish, by will, dated July 7, 1506, proved Sept. 1506, ordered his body to be buried in this chancel. Katherine his testatrix. Legacies are mentioned to John, Thomas, and Edmund, sons of Tho. Hussey, jun. and Eliz. his wife.

"On the S. side of the chancel, on a tablet, to which is fastened a printed paper, in capitals, is a long Latin inscription, almost defaced, in memory of Robert Hayes, who was educated at Winchester, was fellow of New College, Oxford, and rector of this church; who died 30 Novemb. A.D. 1624, aet. 29. This was placed here by his successor, William Wake, of Cambridge. Here are no other inscriptions, marks of brass plates, or painted glass. Here does not appear to have been any church-yard, or indeed any room for one.

"The Register began 1587, but was burnt in the late fire, 1762, as were those of the other parishes, and Arne."

The 14th century

According to Hutchins' account a church must have stood on this site since at least the 12th century, but nothing of that date now remains as the earlier church was replaced by the present one in the 14th century. The combined nave and chancel are of this period, and there must have been originally a contemporary north aisle as the two bay arcade still remains. The most easterly of the two arches has since been rebuilt in segmental form, but the west arch, pointed and of sunk quadrant hollow chamfer and wave mouldings, is original and springs from an octagonal column with a moulded capital, and a semi-octagonal pyramidal corbel bracket on the west respond. A similar corbel which supported the original east arch

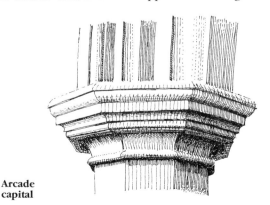

Arcade capital

still remains on the east respond. Other surviving 14th century features include the pointed south doorway with continuous ogee-hollow chamfer-ogee mouldings, two south windows flanking it, each of two cinquefoiled lights in a square head, the pointed rear arch of the later east

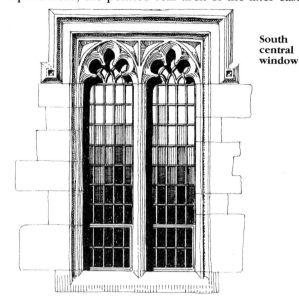

South central window

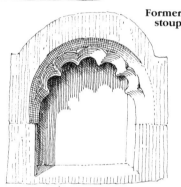

Former stoup

Piscina

window, a piscina in the chancel with a cinquefoiled head in a square outer moulding, and a septfoil headed recess in the porch which would have originally contained a stoup. The south east window, of two cinquefoiled ogee headed lights and glazed spandrels in a square head, is probably of later 14th century date, and the jambs and mullions externally are rebated for former shutters, the cusping at the heads of the lights being also set back in order to accommodate them.

South east window

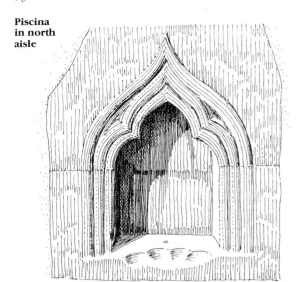

Piscina
in north
aisle

The 15th and 16th centuries

A piscina in the east respond of the north arcade with a trefoiled head and octfoil bowl is of 15th century date, and at the end of the same century or early in the 16th the eastern arch of the north arcade was for some reason rebuilt in its present segmental form with hollow chamfered edges, and is somewhat awkwardly stilted off the central column.

The west tower, added in the late 16th or early 17th century, is plain, without buttresses and divided into two stages with a plain parapet having obelisk shaped pinnacles at the angles and mid points. The belfry windows, one in each face of the upper stage, are single four centre headed lights in square heads, and the west window is of three plain square-headed lights. A similar two light window of about the same date occurs in the north wall of the nave. The tower arch is semi-circular, lightly chamfered, and springs from plain jambs.

The 17th and 18th centuries

The font, now in St Mary's church, is octagonal, and is inscribed 'HF FS TC 1620 CHVRCHWARDENS'. The

The
font

continuous roof of the nave and chancel has a high segmental plastered barrel ceiling with three longitudinal ribs, and is divided into three bays by old tie beams, now reinforced by steel channels fixed to the undersides. The ceiling is probably of 18th century origin, and was probably associated with partial rebuilding of the east wall which includes a plain pointed untraceried window which presumably replaced an original 14th century one. The north aisle seems also to have been rebuilt during the 18th century.

Hutchins (1st edition: 1774) states that the church had remained disused after the fire in 1762, and the situation remained the same in 1796 as the editors of the second edition merely repeat the words of the first edition apart from a modified phrase concerning the tower: "lately containing four bells, three of which, by an order of vestry, were taken down in the year 1784, to be re-cast with those of St Mary's for St Mary's church."

The 19th and 20th centuries

Early in the 19th century the building was being used as a school, although it does not appear to have been properly adapted as such or even put into a good state of repair to judge from Sir Stephen Glynne's notes after a visit on 7 October 1825: "Wareham, Trinity Church is used as a school, and is a very picturesque object from the quantity of ivy which grows up it... and the whole is now in a state of extreme dirt and dilapidation." However, it must have been ultimately adapted and repaired, for Hutchins' editors (3rd edition: 1861) observed: "This church has for some time been occupied as a school, and ... is admirably adapted for school premises." It was finally given up for this purpose in 1886 when the pupils moved into the new Rodgett School in Bonnetts Lane.

When members of the Dorset Natural History and Archaeological Society visited the church on 18 June 1891 (DNHAS Proceedings Vol. 13, p xxvi – xxvii) it was described as: "an historic building whose venerable walls are now coloured blue, and devoted to the useful purpose of a mission chapel," being used as "a meeting place for religious or secular purposes." Later in the present century, after a spell of disuse, it was again repaired, and in 1973 was imaginatively adapted to its present use as the Trinity Art Gallery.

Wareham
(St. Martin)

THERE ARE only eight churches in Dorset which still retain any visible pre-conquest work insitu, mostly confined to isolated sections of structure incorporated into, or as at Studland largely encased in, later work, but here at Wareham St Martin is the most complete Saxon church in the county.

The 11th century

Although the church has been subsequently enlarged and altered, the original characteristically high proportioned nave and chancel remain basically intact, and are of comparable dimensions and proportions to those of the well known Saxon church at Bradford on Avon, Wiltshire. Moreover, as at Bradford on Avon, St Martin's appears also to have been originally ornamented externally by blind wall arcading, as in the upper part of the north wall of the nave, now within the north aisle above the west respond of the arcade, can be seen the

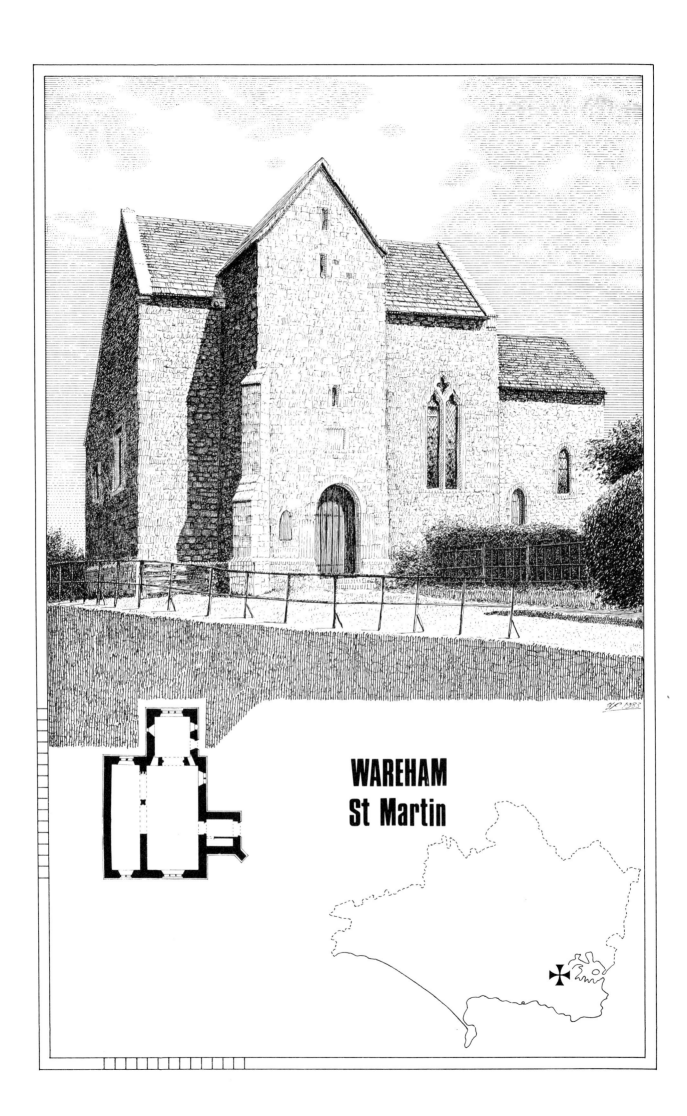

WAREHAM
St Martin

WAREHAM St MARTIN development

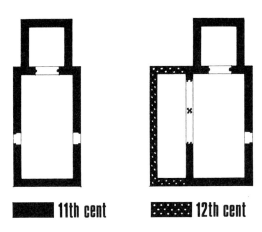

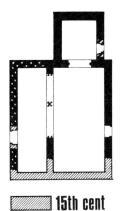

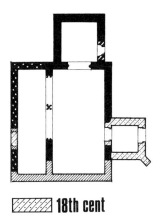

▪▪▪▪ 11th cent   ▦▦▦ 12th cent   ▨▨ 15th cent   ▨▨ 18th cent

base and impost of a pilaster forming part of such arcading, the rest of which was hacked away, so making the wall thinner, when the 12th century arcade was formed.

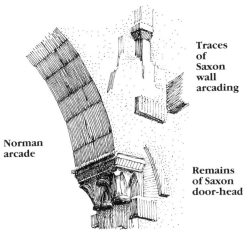

Norman
arcade

Traces
of
Saxon
wall
arcading

Remains
of Saxon
door-head

Below this point, the Norman builders economically made use of the western jamb of the original north doorway to form the west respond of their arcade, and even left in a part of the semi-circular door head which still remains visible from the north aisle. Other surviving features include a small round headed window in the north wall of the chancel, the remains of another subsequently widened in the south wall opposite, and the chancel arch which is semi-circular and plain with a continuous central half round roll moulding interrupted by chamfered imposts carried round as capitals at the springing. There is a roll moulded label on the nave side where the imposts of the arch continue to form a string

course along the east wall, although the south section has since been cut away. Externally the eastern angles of the nave and chancel remain virtually undisturbed, and include some characteristic Saxon long-and-short work particularly noticeable at the north east corner of the nave where the 12th century aisle was simply butted up to the original quoin without any apparent bonding.

The 12th century

Early in the 12th century an altar recess was formed in the east wall of the nave on the south side of the chancel arch, when the original string course was cut away to accommodate it, and although the recess has since been modified and pierced through to form a squint, the round arched head still remains. Towards the end of the 12th century a narrow north aisle was added, and the height of the nave permitted it to be roofed by the simple expedient of extending the north slope of the nave roof. In other churches where narrow 12th century aisles were added to earlier naves (eg Bere Regis and Charminster), although the arcades still remain, the aisles themselves have largely or completely disappeared in the course of subsequent enlargements, but here at St Martin's the original arrangement uniquely still survives. The arcade consists of two plain semi-circular arches springing from stiff leaf foliage carved capitals, originally on a central pier with four free standing round perimeter shafts with matching half column responds, but only the east respond now remains complete. The shafts of the west respond have been since removed, and the central column was rebuilt in its present square panelled form in the 18th century, but the original base remains loose in the church.

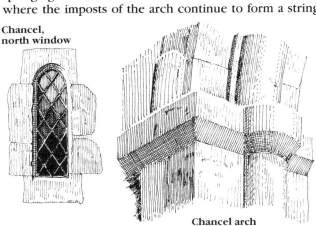

Chancel,
north window

Chancel arch

North
arcade
capital

The completion of the 12th century work was marked by painted consecration crosses on the internal plasterwork, two of which, on the north walls of the nave and chancel still remain. These appear to have formed part of a general scheme of internal wall painting and decoration, some of which remarkably still remains to include an indented pattern on the string course on the east wall of the nave, and most notably, on the north wall of the chancel, two scenes depicting St Martin giving his cloak to a poor beggar. Originally the paintings probably extended over all the internal wall faces of the chancel, as traces of further figures appear on the adjacent window splay and eastern part of the wall, but the remainder have disappeared through subsequent alterations.

The 13th century

Late in the 13th century a pointed and continuously chamfered priest's doorway was inserted in the south wall of the chancel, and the adjacent original window was widened to its present lancet form. These works would have disturbed any original wall painting on the south side of the chancel and probably prompted a scheme of internal re-decoration when the earlier scenes appear to have been over-painted by a simpler arrangement of masonry lining with marginal patterns of lozenge, leaf and scroll motifs. At the same time the nave seems to have been redecorated in the same vein, as similar masonry lining and motifs still remain on the chancel arch and north arcade.

The 14th century

Work of this period seems to have been concentrated solely in the south east corner of the nave where a window of two trefoiled ogee headed lights, rebated externally for shutters, with an ogival quatrefoil tracery light, was inserted in the south wall. Nearby in the east

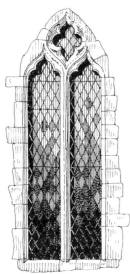

South window of nave

wall the earlier altar recess was blocked, and between it and the chancel arch a niche was formed with a trefoiled round head. In the north aisle there is a piscina bowl unusually shaped in the form of a regular trapezium which may be of 13th or 14th century date.

The 15th century

When the church was first built, North Street which passes close to the west end, must have been at a much higher level than at present, and it would have reached its present level of ten feet or more below the churchyard by a process of gradual erosion over the centuries. By the 15th century this process must have reached a point where the structural stability of the church was being

seriously threatened, when it appears to have been necessary to rebuild the whole of the west end, presumably on deeper foundations. The whole of the west wall, including a return portion at the south end, is of this period and includes a window of three trefoiled lights in a square head in the west wall of the nave. In accordance with normal 15th century practice the natural lighting of the interior was increased by replacing original small windows by much larger ones, and two vertical traceried windows were inserted in the east walls of the north aisle and chancel, of two and three lights respectively. This

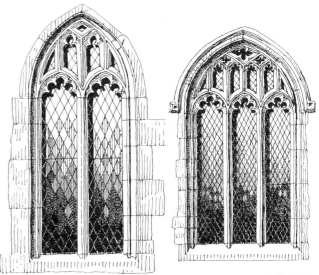

Chancel, east window　　　**North aisle, east window**

work must have again seriously disrupted the earlier 12th and 13th century internal wall decorations which seem to have been once more adapted and overpainted to some extent. Remaining wall painting of this period includes an indented pattern on the rear arch of the east window of the chancel, roses on the associated east wall, a crowned IHS monogram on the north wall of the chancel, a pattern of stars on the east wall of the nave and part of a black letter inscription on the west wall. Other 15th century items include a pair of image brackets flanking the east window in the north aisle, the north doorway of the aisle which has since been blocked, and a ridge tile from the roof having a socket for a former gable cross.

The 16th century

The roofs of the nave and north aisle appear to have been renewed in their original positions at this time as the present exposed rafter roofs, presumably of 1935-36, incorporate parts of 16th century principals. The roof of the north aisle is divided into three bays by cambered beams with raking struts, and that of the nave is divided into four unequal bays by queen post tie beam trusses which incorporate some old timber members. The west window of the north aisle, of two plain square headed lights, is also of 16th century date.

Further wall paintings were added during the 16th, 17th, and 18th centuries, mostly in the form of black letter texts, now mostly fragmentary and overlying some of the earlier painted plasterwork, producing in places an interesting, if confusing, succession of layers one upon another. An early 17th century text running around the chancel arch is from St Paul's espistle to the Romans (chapter 13, verse 1), and although now some parts are missing, it originally read: "Let every soul be subject unto the higher powers. For there is no power but of God."

The fascinating interior of St Martin's containing an amalgamation of architectural features spanning almost 900 years from the 11th century chancel arch to the 20th century effigy of Lawrence of Arabia
[Photograph: Colin Graham]

The 17th century

The principal survival of this period is the font which consists of a plain octagonal bowl set against the west respond of the north arcade and supported in a rather undignified manner by two plain slabs of stone standing on end. An inscription on the bowl, in four lines with some of the words randomly split between them, records that it was:

SET UP BY WILLI
AM WELSTED
AND PHILIP HEL
LIAR 1607

The font

The 18th century

Hutchins (1st edition: 1774) states that: "On the south is a high porch serving for a tower, built 1712, in which is one small bell," and a stone panel above the entrance arch is inscribed "RICHARd COOLE EdWARd BENET CHORCH WARd ANS 1712". Although the tower could be considered to detract from the simple form of the original Saxon church, it nevertheless makes a pleasing composition from the south and contributes to the distinctive character of this church. It has a round headed entrance arch, small randomly placed openings in the form of loop lights, a diagonal two stage buttress at the south west angle and a gabled roof. This work on the tower was closely followed by yet another addition to the internal wall painting when a royal arms of Queen Anne, dated 1713, was painted above the chancel arch.

Hutchins (1st edition: 1774) records that: "Since the union of the church (in 1678) it was, in winter time, officiated in every Sunday morning, afterwards only once a-month, and about 1736 disused, except for marriages, christenings, and churching of women." After the fire of 1762 the church was used to accommodate some of the poorer people whose homes had been destroyed, and

various adaptations were made including the installation of a fireplace, the chimney of which still remains in the north aisle. Hutchins' editors (2nd edition: 1815) give the cost of the adaptations as £1. 10s. 9d., made up of: "The bricklayer's bill 15s. 9d.; carpenter's 7s. 6d.; glazier's 7s. 6d."

The 19th century

For the remainder of the 18th century and during the whole of the 19th the building remained disused and derelict, with a sanded floor and most of the windows bricked up, no doubt survivals from its residential use after the fire, and the walls externally became shrouded in ivy. Yet in spite of (or perhaps because of) such a long period of decay and neglect the building has survived; no doubt if it had remained in use as a church there would have been a thorough Victorian restoration when many of the old features which still remain would have been ruthlessly swept away. Hutchins' editors (3rd edition: 1861) referred to its condition at that time: "As a place of religious assemblage it is now entirely deserted, and, unless speedy efforts are made for its preservation, it will be impossible to prevent its complete ruin... Beneath the decaying whitewash the walls appear covered with texts of scripture and pious admonitions."

The 20th century

When members of the Dorset Natural History and Archaeological Society visited the church on 27 July 1907 (Proceedings Vol. 28, p lxvii - lxviii) it was observed: "The barn-like roof, the riven rent in the walls, and the floor of sand, together with a general air of forsaken neglect, give to the place a very extraordinary yet interesting effect." The church remained in this condition until 1935-36 when a carefully considered scheme of conservation and repair works was carried out, so that after 200 years of disuse as a church it was re-dedicated by the bishop on 23 November 1936, as recorded on a commemorative plate in the entrance porch, since when it has remained in use for occasional services.

A notable 20th century item is a recumbent effigy of T. E. Lawrence (1888-1935), the famous Lawrence of Arabia who is buried at Moreton. The monument is of Purbeck stone and inscribed: 'Carved by Eric Kennington 1935-9'.

St Martin's in 1814 from a watercolour by J. B. Knight

[Source: Dorset County Museum collection]

Wareham
(St. Mary)

EARLY IN the 8th century three large and important churches are known to have been established in Dorset – Wimborne, founded by St Cuthberga, sister of King Ina of Wessex (688-726), and Sherborne and Wareham, both founded by St Aldhelm (c639-709). At Sherborne and Wimborne surviving pre-conquest work is limited to comparatively isolated portions incorporated into several subsequent rebuilding schemes, but at Wareham St Mary the complete nave and aisles of the original 8th century church survived remarkably complete until 1841 when they were demolished and rebuilt in their present form. But for this regrettable destruction, Wareham St Mary would be the largest and most impressive Saxon building in Britain, as is clearly shown by a plan of the old building drawn in 1840 shortly before its demolition.

The 8th century

Christian churches originated in Rome when the early Christians there made use of redundant Roman halls of justice, known as basilicas. These buildings, consisting of a nave and aisles with a semi-circular apse at one end (where the presiding justices seated against its walls all faced the accused person), seem to have been particularly well suited to early Christian patterns of worship to the extent that this basic plan form was adopted for newly built churches all over Europe for many centuries afterwards. There can be no doubt that the original 8th century church here at Wareham was of this basilican form, particularly when compared to the contemporary church at Brixworth, Northamptonshire, where the original nave and arcades, west tower, presbytery and reconstructed apse still survive. The aisles at Brixworth have disappeared but the foundations of the north aisle have been excavated to reveal a plan form of remarkable similarity to that of the early Wareham church, to the extent that the original arrangements of the east and west ends rebuilt at Wareham during the 14th to 16th centuries can be deduced with a reasonable degree of certainty. Moreover 12th and 13th century additions appear also to have followed a similar pattern at both

churches where south chapels were added to the square presbyteries, enabling the eastward extent of the original Wareham presbytery to be deduced. At Brixworth there was a ring crypt, or external ambulatory, around the outside of the apse and this is likely also to have been a feature of Wareham, whilst at the west end there would have been a narthex formed by a central tower-like feature flanked by porches, as at Brixworth where the tower component still remains. At Sherborne, founded by St Aldhelm at about the same time, recent excavation has shown there to have been a similar arrangement originally at the west end. At Brixworth remaining responds and excavation below the floor show that the presbytery was originally separated from the nave by an arcade of three arches, and as this is likely to have been the original arrangement at Wareham also, the wide span semi-circular chancel arch which remained until 1841 was probably a later, 12th century reconstruction.

As with the basilican plan form, Roman methods of design and construction persisted long after the demise of the Roman empire, and this influence can be clearly detected in the plan, drawings and descriptions of the old nave and aisles. The arcades were formed of plain semi-circular arches with substantial sections of walling between them, and the aisles were divided into comparable bays by similar arches at right angles to those of the arcades, forming a mutually buttressing and inherently stable system of construction which appears to have remained sound in 1841 after more than 1100 years. Pre-1841 drawings of the exterior of the old church reveal further striking similarities with Brixworth where the high nave clerestory walls with tall and narrow round headed windows which still remain are almost identical to those which formerly existed at Wareham. Although of comparable sizes, the plans of Brixworth and Wareham differed in one respect – whereas at Brixworth the nave arcades are in four bays, at Wareham they were in six, a central bay of the north aisle being in the form of an entrance porch gabled to the north, with a further external door in the south aisle opposite where according

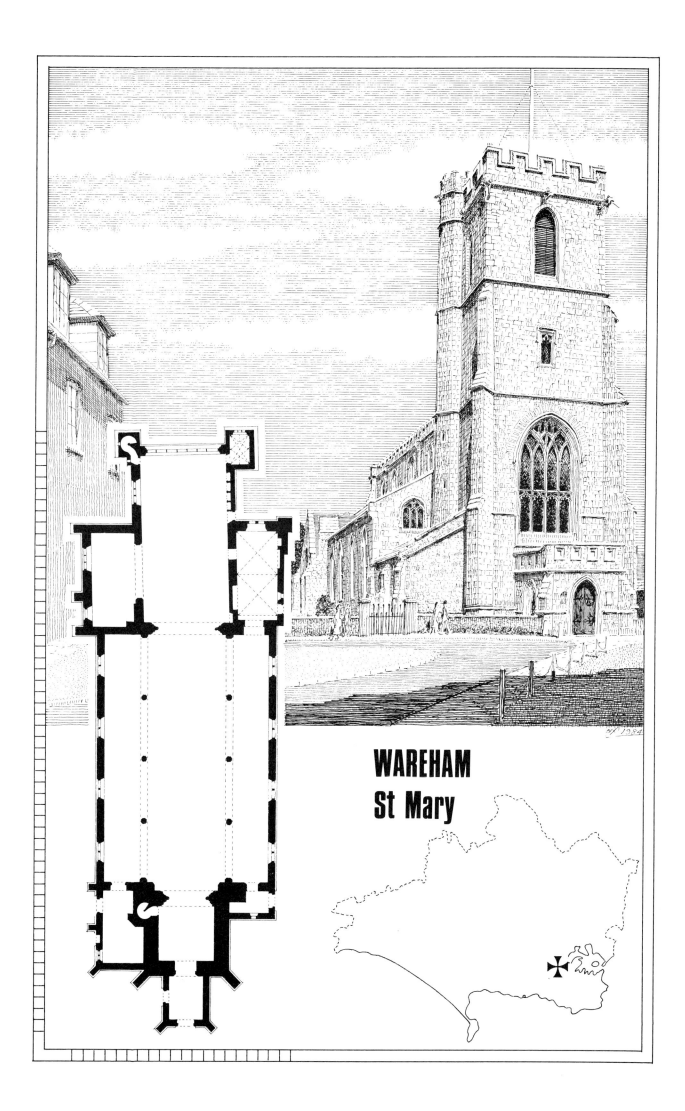

WAREHAM
St Mary

WAREHAM St MARY development

■■■ 8th cent (partly conjectural)

▒▒▒ 12th cent

▓▓▓ 14th cent ░░░ 15th cent ⊠⊠⊠ 16th cent

⠄⠄⠄ 19th cent

to Hutchins (1st edition: 1774) there was evidence of a former porch similar to that on the north side.

Perhaps the most intriguing aspect of the old church was the discovery of five inscribed stones, now on display in the present building, which came to light during the course of demolition in 1841. They record burials of early Christians having names of Celtic origin, and based on the style of lettering, are considered to range in date from the 7th to the early 9th centuries, and although some may be contemporary with or slightly later in date than the early 8th century church, two of them may pre-date it and suggest the existence of an even earlier church or at least an earlier Christian cemetery. In chronological order the inscriptions are as follows:

1. VIDCV ... FILIUS VIDA ...
2. IUDNNE ... FIL . QUI ...
3. CATGUG C ... FILIUS GIDEO
4. DENIEL FILIUS ... AUPRIT IACET
5. GONGORIE

Although the rebuilding of 1841-42 involved complete demolition of the original nave and aisles, the west walls of the present aisles are in the same position as formerly and may still retain some original walling. Likewise the east wall of the north aisle adjoining the organ chamber is also in its original position so that it too may consist basically of 8th century work, although in all three cases plaster obscures any evidence there might be of early masonry. Other pre-conquest remains include fragments of a Saxon cross shaft and a cross head.

The 12th century

Early in the 12th century St Edward's chapel was added on the south side of the original presbytery, and if as is probable it took the same form as a 13th century chapel added in an exactly similar position at Brixworth, its length from east to west would have been governed by the length of the rectangular presbytery. Most of the features of the chapel are of later date, but the original wall structure survives to include a shallow clasping buttress at the north east angle, a half round string course moulding in the east wall externally, and the archway to the south aisle which is semi-circular and of one plain order springing from moulded imposts. The western section of the south wall is thinner than the remainder, suggesting that it was originally an internal wall, consistent with this portion having been linked to the remaining priory buildings lying to the south, perhaps in the form of cloisters.

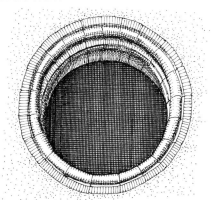

Round window

A round window with a roll moulded surround in the east wall of the north aisle, now opening to the organ chamber, is a rare 12th century item which may have originally formed part of St Edward's chapel, possibly the former east window before being replaced by the present 13th century one. A later 12th century pointed doorway

with head and jambs carved with shallow chevron and nail head enrichment has been reset at high level in the south wall of the chancel at the west end. The most unusual 12th century item is the hexagonal lead font bowl, each of its sides being ornamented by a pair of semi-circular arches supported on fluted columns, each enclosing a standing figure, twelve in all, undoubtedly representing the twelve apostles, as St Peter holding a key is instantly recognisable. There are said to be 38 lead fonts in England altogether and Wareham's is unique in being the only hexagonal one among them.

The font

The 13th century

Another unusual aspect of the font is that its base, of Purbeck stone and marble with angle shafting, is not only of a differing shape, being octagonal rather than hexagonal to match the bowl, but is of a later, 13th century date, and presumably replaced an earlier base.

Early in the 13th century St Edward's chapel was considerably altered to its present two storey form by the insertion of a floor supported by simple quadripartite vaulting with chamfered ribs springing from detached Purbeck marble shafts, and having recessed rib intersections carved with foliage devices. At the same time the original east window was replaced by the present one which is an interesting early example of plate tracery

St Edward's chapel, east window

in the form of a pair of lancets with a central quatrefoil above. There are remains of a further window in the wall above, perhaps of a similar type, which would have lit the upper chamber. There is also a contemporary piscina in the chapel with an unusual head in the form of an irregular quatrefoil with a keystone, and a further piscina, now reset in the east wall of the north aisle, has a trefoiled head and a projecting double rounded bowl supported on semi-conical corbels. Other items of this period include a late 13th century tomb recess with a cinquefoil cusped

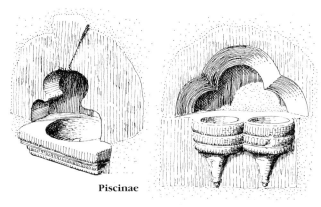

Piscinae

St Edward's chapel as depicted in volume 1 of Hutchins's 2nd edition (1796) showing the two effigies in their original positions

arched head in the north wall of St Edward's chapel, several broken stone coffins in the churchyard, parts of stone coffin lids, and one complete, large and very fine boat shaped stone coffin in the north aisle. Although probably of 13th century date, it has long been associated traditionally with the burial of King Edward the Martyr who was assassinated at Corfe in 978 and buried initially at Wareham before his body was later borne in state to Shaftesbury abbey. St Edward's chapel, dedicated to him, is traditionally believed to have been built on the site of his burial, and this stone coffin is said to have been discovered under the chapel floor.

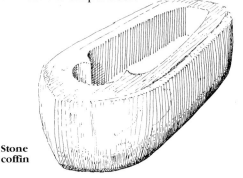

Stone coffin

On either side of the chancel are two notable recumbent effigies of knights attributed to Sir Henry d'Estoke (literally 'of East Stoke') who died about 1240, and Sir William d'Estoke who died in 1294. These effigies were originally in St Edward's chapel as recorded by

Hutchins (1st edition: 1774), and Dr. G. Dru Drury, writing in DNHAS Proceedings (Vol. 60, pp 90-94) described them in some detail, remarking that: "The earlier Figure is the largest and finest military effigy in Dorset, and indeed ranks amongst the best examples of its period and style in the whole country."

The 14th century

During the first half of the 14th century, whatever may have remained of the original presbytery and apse was taken down and replaced by a chancel of imposing dimensions, originally 60 feet long but shortened in 1841-42 by extending the nave eastwards. It was thus comparable in dimensions to the chancels at Sherborne and Wimborne, and moreover the work was, and still remains, of high architectural quality. The east window is immense, occupying almost the whole of the east wall, and is divided into seven trefoil headed lights with transomes below reticulated tracery in a four centred head. The structural implications of such a large window

Henry and William d'Estoke

Chancel east window

are catered for by huge buttresses at the eastern angles, that on the north side containing a stair turret to the roof, whilst the lower part of the south east buttress contains within it a small chapel dedicated to St Thomas à Becket, having a lierne vaulted roof with moulded ribs and carved bosses. Of the three original windows on the north side of the chancel, one disappeared as a result of the 1841-42 rebuilding, but two remain, one having been re-used in the north wall of the 19th century organ chamber. They are both of three lights and have characteristically diverse tracery, one being of open cusped roundel form and the other with more complex and flowing sub-divisions. On

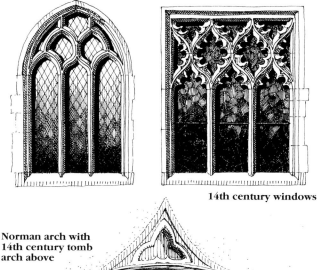

14th century windows

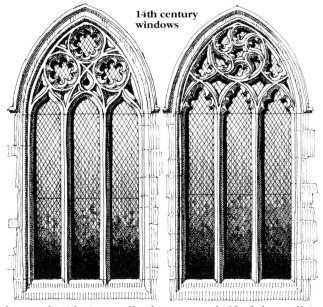

14th century windows

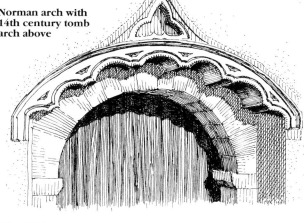

Norman arch with 14th century tomb arch above

the south side internally the eastern half of the wall is largely occupied by a priest's door and a fine four bay sedilia of four centred arches springing from triple shafts, the bases of the recesses forming seats stepped up towards the east, with a double piscina in the eastern bay.

The 15th century

During most of this period no major alterations appear to have been undertaken as surviving items are confined to windows and other relatively small features. These include a window of three cinquefoiled lights with vertical tracery in a pointed head in the south wall of the chancel, a similar but much smaller window in the east

Sedilia

Becket chapel, east window

Chancel, south window

Although the 14th century work was concentrated in the new chancel, minor alterations and embellishments were evidently carried out in other parts of the building, as two windows reset at high level in the west walls of the aisles are of this period. They are both of unusual design, that on the north side being of three plain lights with uncusped curvilinear tracery in a pointed head, whilst the south window is of three cinquefoiled lights with octfoiled tracery lights under a square head. Other remains of this period include a stone panel carved with the Crucifixion now reset on the east wall of the north aisle, and a septfoiled segmental arched head from a former tomb recess now reset over the entrance to St Edward's chapel. It is almost identical to one in Bere Regis church which still serves its original purpose.

wall of the Becket chapel which must have replaced an earlier 14th century one, and another similar but uncusped window in the east wall of the north aisle now unglazed and forming a sound aperture from the organ chamber. Other items include a piscina with a trefoiled ogee head in the Becket chapel, a stoup in the north west vestry, and among an assembly of stone items and fragments in the north aisle, parts of an octagonal font or cross base, parts of a trefoil panelled stoup, parts of a carving of the Crucifixion, and quatrefoil panelling probably from a former table tomb.

Late in the 15th century the present west tower was added on the site of the original narthex arrangement forming the west front, part of which may well have survived until then. It is of four stages with square set buttresses at the east angles and diagonal ones to the west with an octagonal stair turret near the north east angle, and there are grotesque gargoyles at the angles and mid points of the upper string course below an embattled parapet which originally had pinnacles at the angles. Hutchins' editors (3rd edition: 1861) say: "Not many years since this tower was damaged in a thunder-storm, the electric current loosening several large stones, which led to the removal of the pinnacles then surmounting the angles." The original tracery has been removed from the belfry windows which are now plainly louvred, except on the east side where the lower part of the central mullion remains together with a transome forming cinquefoil headed sub-lights. The original tracery of the west window has also been removed and replaced by 19th century intersecting tracery. Evidently the slightly later west porch was an afterthought as a cinquefoil headed recess above the west doorway is partially obscured by the roof. Internally the tower arch is tall, pointed and of ogee-wave-ogee mouldings, the inner represented on the jambs by attached shafts with moulded capitals, the middle order continuous, and the outer interrupted by capitals.

The 16th century

Shortly after the west tower was completed a chapel and porch were added to the north and west sides of it, and both these additions show early evidence of approaching Renaissance developments in that the parapets, instead of being embattled, are ornamented by recessed panels, although those of the raking parapet of the chapel are now partly missing. An original north window of the chapel is of two cinquefoiled ogee headed lights in a square head and the adjoining doorway, since blocked, is pointed under a square head forming spandrels carved with quatrefoils enclosing a Tudor rose and patera. A Tudor rose also occurs on the base of a niche above it which has a gabled and trefoiled head between side standards.

This early 16th century work at the west end may also have included the provision of a similar chapel on the south side of the tower, forming a symmetrical arrangement, as Hutchins observed with reference to the south aisle: "At the lower end of this isle seems to have been another chapel, on the S. side of the tower; where foundations of a building plainly appear, and a door leading out of the isle." On the other hand the old foundations which Hutchins saw could have been the remains of the south end of the original narthex which would have extended beyond the present tower.

The 17th century

Items of this period include the communion table in St Edward's chapel, which is ornamented with gadroon and strapwork motifs and has legs carved as winged lions, two panelled and carved chairs, one dated 1650, and a carved and panelled chest dated 1687. There are also five inscribed memorial brasses commemorating Anne Franke 1583, William Perkins 1613, Richard Perkins 1616, Edmund Moore 1625 and George Burges 1640.

The 18th century

By the 18th century when semi-circular arches and other Renaissance classical idioms had become firmly established, the old 8th century nave and aisles built 1000 years previously with strongly marked and original classical influences, would have been peculiarly in accord with the architectural taste and fashion of that time, providing an ideal setting for a general scheme of refurbishment and refitting. In fact such was the affinity between the old structure and the 18th century fittings, that in the 19th century the nave and aisles were widely considered to be entirely of the 18th century and consequently of little or no interest. The pair of doors with fielded panels in the west doorway is all that now survives from this period, but Hutchins (1st edition: 1774) refers to several other items:

"The chancel was formerly separated from the choir by a large wooden screen, removed 1720; ... at the E. end is a very large noble window, one third of which is now walled up... Over the arch that leads into the choir, is the king's arms curiously done in stucco, and set up at the expense of the parish, 1745. On the S. side of the upper end of the nave is a gallery, and another on the N. side. The nave and choir are paved with stone cut in a diamond form... The church was new paved and seated, 1745; the arches and pillars repaired, the roof ceiled, and the W. window glazed... The isles were ceiled, 1751; the N. gallery built, 1762."

The editors of the 2nd edition of 1796 record later 18th century works, including the recasting of bells:

"By an order of vestry, September 29, 1784, the same were taken down, and, with the bells from Trinity church, re-cast into a set of eight bells, total weight of metal seventy-five hundred weight three quarters nine pounds, at the expense of £290. 4s. 10d. to which John Calcroft, esq contributed a donation of £50 and the inhabitants of St Mary's parish the residue. These bells are very musical, and are heard at a considerable distance; their melody is much softened from the contiguity of the tower to the river Frome.

"Martha Turner, widow, late of this town, by her will, bequeathed £100 to the rector of Wareham for an altar piece in the parish church of Lady St Mary and the same has been since erected in wainscot, in the Doric order, and is seventeen feet and a quarter, broad and thirteen feet high. On a black ground, on four tables, are the Lord's Prayer, the Creed, and Ten Commandments, in gold letters; and over all the followng inscription: 'This altar-piece was the gift of Martha, widow of George Turner, of Penleigh, in the county of Wilts, esq., and only child of Anthony Trew, gentleman, late of this town.' She died in January 1789 at Wareham."

The 19th century

This series of 18th century refitting and furnishing schemes seems to have continued into the early part of the 19th century as there is a recorded faculty of 1811 for the erection of a further gallery. The need for additional accommodation continued to increase until 1840 when the dilapidated and dangerous state of the roof led to the disastrous decision to rebuild the whole of the nave and aisles. Those most concerned with this decision seem to have been totally unaware of the age of the building and of its unique architectural importance, but perhaps surprisingly for the time, one inhabitant recognising the building's importance, was moved to write to the Dorset County Chronicle making a plea for its preservation. His letter headed "Wareham, 26th August, 1840," and signed with the pseudonym "Antiquarius," was published in the

Two interesting views of the church before the rebuilding of the nave and aisles in 1841-42. The watercolours are of 1864 but based on earlier sketches

[Source: Wareham, Lady St Mary Church]

issue of 3 September 1840:

" ... as this is a very ancient structure I cannot but express a feeling of regret that reports are in circulation of a design to pull down part of the vnerable fabric, and to increase the number of sittings and render it more convenient and comfortable, not with due regard to the interesting features of the structure, but by some dovetailing of a modern character. As this essential object could be attained without the comtemplated sacrifice, in the multiplicity of opinions some plan appears desirable that should avoid the rushing into the enormous expense which so sweeping a measure would entail, I am induced to request the favour of your allowing me a corner in your much read publication, to enter a protest against such sacrilegious demolition. The immediate cause of agitation at the present time arises from the dangerous state of the roof, which is so dilapidated as to require complete renewal. The span of the roof of the nave in its present state is about 25ft., and if new walls were carried up from the foundation of the outer walls of the narrower aisles, (as had been suggested) it would give one roof over the whole span of nearly 40 ft; which, while it would undoubtedly add to the accommodation by providing room for additional galleries, it would at once destroy the character of the building ...

"I own, Sir, that it is very easy to find fault, and if, in my anxiety to rescue from destruction a fabric which has existed for so many centuries, I could not suggest a plausible plan by which increased accommodation could be obtained without so great a sacrifice, I would not have troubled you or your readers with this communication." He then goes on to suggest how the required additional accommodation could be provided by re-siting the organ, and bringing back into use areas under the aisle galleries: "now wholly unappropriated," together with other minor internal re-arrangements. However, the pleas of Antiquarius, whose knowledge and views on historic buildings were some 50 years ahead of his time, went unheeded, and rebuilding of the nave and aisles went ahead, the architect being Professor T. L. Donaldson of London, and the contractors Cornicks of Bridport.

Various issues of the Dorset County Chronicle record the preliminaries and commencement of the work, of which the following are extracts or summaries:

8 October 1840 – The Salisbury Diocesan Church Building Association had approved a grant of £350 "towards extensive enlargement of the Church."

22 October 1840 – An appeal for further subscribers to the rebuilding fund, with a list of subscribers to date. "It is proposed to take down the Nave of the Church and to rebuild it upon an extended scale, so as to contain 995 Sittings, 600 thereof to be FREE for ever, the estimated expense of the undertaking is £2,200. A most munificent grant of £350 has been made by the "Salisbury Diocesan Church Building Association" and valuable aid is contemplated from the Metropolitan Parent Society. The inhabitants of Wareham have already subscribed £500 which with other contributors amounts to the sum of £1,057. 1s. 0d., but a large deficiency will remain unprovided for."

4 February 1841 – "We are glad to report that the subscription for the noble work of rebuilding on an enlarged scale the Venerable Lady St Mary Church of Wareham is now so forward that the Churchwardens have advertised for tenders,

although a considerable sum is still wanting to carry into effect the public spirited intentions of the committee."

6 May 1841 – "The work of taking down and rebuilding the Church of Lady St Mary in this town, commenced on Monday last. The contract has been taken by Messrs. Cornick, of Bridport."

20 May 1841 – "The Committee for the rebuilding of Wareham Church recently met and notwithstanding the present inadequacy of their funds, they resolved to accept the tender of Messrs Cornick of Bridport, confiding in the continued beneficence of a Christian community for the means of completion. The work of demolition has already begun, and many valuable fragments have been found in the walls, with inscriptions of a very curious character which must have formed part of the construction of a former church. Mr Donaldson, the architect, has directed these relics to be preserved for the purpose of being inserted in the new walls in some prominent part."

The work then proceeded, but not without incident. During the late summer of 1841 an anonymous letter writer was active, making allegations that the materials and workmanship were of poor quality, and although this was strenuously denied by the churchwardens and building committee, the diocesan authorities took the allegations seriously enough to call in the diocesan architect T. H. Wyatt to report on the matter. However, Wyatt found no grounds for the allegations and his report, dated 2 October 1841, stated that the work was considered satisfactory. The building committee, delighted with this outcome and anxious to combat the still persistent rumours, at a meeting on 12 October resolved to make these findings as widely known as possible by publishing the Archdeacon's letter on the subject which duly appeared in the advertising columns of the Dorset County Chronicle of 21 October 1841:

"Gentlemen, – I have this morning (6 October) received from Mr Lowther (the Secretary of our Diocesan Church Building Association) the substance of the report of Mr Wyatt on the Works of the Church at Wareham; and I have great pleasure in informing you, and through you, all other parties who may be interested therein, that everything as far as it has proceeded, is quite satisfactory – and that there is no just cause for the calumnious accusations of various kinds, that have been so industriously circulated. The Report will, I feel assured, be a great satisfaction to you, as also to the Architect and Builder. I remain Gentlemen, etc. R. Bentley Buckle, Archdeacon."

This was reinforced by a paragraph elsewhere in the same issue:

"Rebuilding of Wareham Church. We beg to direct attention to our advertising column for an interesting notice respecting the above Church. Some anonymous slanderer had, it seems been writing to the Bishop, endeavouring to injure and retard the progress of the work, and not only to question the ability of the architect and builder, but to reflect on the judgement and discretion of the respected churchwardens, Messrs. Mortimer and Baskett to whose strenuous exertion and unwearied zeal the town is mainly indebted for this great local improvement."

In spite of these reassurances there would appear to have been at least some grounds for the rumours concerning faulty materials and workmanship, as part of

V.I. p.59

NORTH VIEW of St MARY'S CHURCH in WAREHAM.

This Plate is most gratefully   Inscribed to the Donor Mrs Turner,

Relict of George Turner Esq of   Penleigh, in Wiltshire, by the Author.

An 18th century engraving of the church which appeared in Hutchins's 1st edition (1774) and which was also used in the 2nd and 3rd editions of 1796 and 1861

A lithograph of 1821 drawn by S. Prout showing the east end of the church in a very rural looking setting. The top of the tower appears to have been in need of repair and the east window of the chancel was blocked up to transome level to accommodate the 18th century reredos. The tower of Holy Trinity church can be seen in the background

the incomplete work collapsed after a prolonged spell of wet and windy weather. The affected portion seems to have been in the clerestory walling where the failed brickwork was then replaced by solid stonework. At that period of the 19th century when the only available bedding material was plain lime mortar which took a very long time to set and fully harden, freshly laid brickwork unprotected by a roof was particularly vulnerable to heavy rain, and accounts for the fact that 'roofing-in' was considered such a significant occasion and worthy of celebration. Former letters concerning these events have been destroyed, but Alan Sturdy who saw them in 1934 wrote a lengthy and informative article on his recollections of them in DNHAS Proceedings Vol. 62, pp 78-96.

The church was officially re-opened on 29 September 1842, and the following extracts concerning this event and others leading up to it are from the Dorset County Chronicle.

19 May 1842 – "We have to record another instance of the benevolent and Christian feeling of the Dowager Queen Adelaide, Her Majesty having generously contributed the sum of £15 to Wareham Lady St Mary Church – we regret to state that to complete the arduous undertaking of putting into thorough repair and restoring this sacred edifice, several hundred pounds are yet required, but which we hope will be supplied by the liberality of the friends of the Church."

16 June 1842 – "This handsome structure having been within the last week, covered in, and thus far giving satisfaction to the town at large, many of the inhabitants subscribed towards giving the labourers a rearing dinner etc., and on Friday last nearly 40 assembled at the Horse and Groom where a substantial feast was prepared. Mr Cornick junr (The Contractor) Mr Webber, the superintendent, a Clerk of the Works, and several inhabitants joined, and the men separated at a late

hour, much gratified, and grateful to those by whose liberality they had thus been treated."

11 August 1842 – "The rebuilding of Lady St Mary Church is fast drawing towards completion; the scaffolding of the interior has been struck; the ancient window of the chancel, of which a part has been walled up for many years, has been thrown open, and the whole has now assumed a grand appearance. It is expected that in about two months all the work will be finished. The tender of Mr Edginton of Salisbury for laying the pipes and fittings for lighting the church with gas has been accepted; and has also the tender of Mr James Ling of Taunton for repairing and erecting the organ."

6 October 1842 – "The town of Wareham presented a scene of much animation and interest on Thursday last which was appointed for the re-opening of Lady St Mary Church in that ancient place. The bells rang merry peals; the national flag proudly floated upon the church tower, the Town Hall, and other public buildings; carriages and other vehicles were constantly arriving from the surrounding neighbourhood. There was a general stir and appearance of delight among the inhabitants; and everything conspired to show the depth of feeling which prevailed as to the auspiciousness and importance of the event about to take place ... In 1840 the old Church was discovered to be in so dilapidated a state that it was deemed necessary at once to pull it down, and to take advantage of the opportunity of increasing the accommodation, as the 450 sittings which it contained – most of them being incommodious, and many of them unfit for occupation from damp and exposure – were insufficient for the population of Wareham. The old church had these two important features which are still retained, the noble Tower and

spacious Chancel; and the body of the church consisted of a nave and two side aisles divided from the latter by cumbrous square piers which impeded the sight and hearing, and occupied great space. It was evident that this portion of the fabric had been rebuilt within a couple of centuries as it differed so materially in the character of its architectural design from the tower and chancel, which were doubtless erected during the finest period of chaste Gothic architecture. The alterations having been determined upon, that intelligent and talented architect, Mr Donaldson of London, was selected for effecting the object which notwithstanding untoward circumstances causing delay over which he had no control, has been, at length happily completed to the entire satisfaction of the Parishioners upon his judicious plan, which has been well adapted to the means at hand; and it is no small praise to that gentleman considering all the circumstances that the extras had not carried the expense very much beyond the original estimate. It is also due to the respectable clerk of the works, Mr Henry Webber to notice that his ability and exertions have tended much to facilitate the progress and satisfactory completion of the work. The contractors for this are Messrs. Cornick of Bridport."

The report then goes on to describe the new work and the consecration service itself. As the economic state of the country at any given period is invariably reflected in its architecture, 1841, coming within the period often referred to as the 'hungry forties', cannot be regarded as a very good year in that respect, and consequently the nave and aisles of 1841-42 are generally considered, with much justification, to be dull and unimaginative. In addition the interior effect is somewhat bare and austere, but this is almost entirely due to the subsequent removal of the aisle galleries which were an integral part of the original design, the much more satisfactory original proportions being evident in an old photograph of the interior taken before the galleries were removed in 1903.

The nave and aisles are in four coincident structural bays without buttresses, with tall aisle windows each of two plain pointed lights with straight transomes and uncusped open vertical tracery in pointed heads, whilst above them the aisles have plain eaves. Above the slated lean-to roofs of the aisles the nave clerestories have

embattled parapets and clerestory windows, one per bay, each of two plain lights with a tracery quatrefoil in a pointed head. Internally the arcades are formed of pointed arches of two lightly chamfered orders springing from tall octagonal columns, all with a plastered finish except the moulded capitals of the columns which are in Ham Hill stone. The original roofs of the nave and aisles have since been renewed, but the chancel roof of 1841-42 still remains. It is of exposed boarding and rafters divided into six bays by arch braced principals with iron tie rods and shaped stub beams at the feet braced from wall posts and supported by semi-octagonal stone corbels.

Work of the first half of the 19th century, which included box pews and other internal fittings based on 18th century traditions, was generally much disliked during the latter half of the century, and accordingly a faculty dated 9 May 1882 was for a general restoration concerned principally with replacement of internal fittings at an estimated cost of £1590 (almost two thirds of the cost of the 1841-42 rebuilding), the architects being John Colson and Sons of Winchester. It was proposed to:

"... take down and remove the screen and partition between the Tower and Nave of the said Church; to remove and refix the Prayer Desk and Pulpit placing the former near the north eastern corner of the Chancel and the latter near the south western corner of such Chancel, to reglaze the western window in the Tower; to remove the said Western Gallery; to lengthen the Northern and Southern Galleries at the western ends thereof and remove the whole of the seats and fittings of such Galleries and entirely reseat and refit the same, to remove the panelling to the fronts of such Galleries and renew the same, to repair the Staircases leading to such Galleries, to remove the present gas fittings erected in the said Nave, Aisles and Galleries and provide and fix new ones; to remove the whole of the paving, floors, seats and fittings of the Nave and North and South Aisles of the said Church, and entirely repave, refloor, reseat and refit the same... to provide and fix in the Chancel of the said Church at the east end thereof a Reredos formed of oak." The work also included external excavations and the provision of new drains and gutters and the installation of a new heating system. From the specification the work was to be commenced on 15 May 1882, and: "completed and finished fit for the performance of Divine Service by the 1st day of September 1882". There was a penalty of £5 per week for non-completion by the stipulated date, but in the

The interior before the galleries were removed in 1903. The photograph, which was used to support the 1903 faculty application, had been taken by Mrs W. H. Huddleston of Wareham

event of additional works the contract would be: "extended one week for every extra £25 worth of works".

The present organ, by Maley, Young and Oldknow of London, was presented to the church by Mrs Rodgett of Sandford in memory of her husband Miles Rodgett who died on 6 June 1882. Initially it was placed at the east end of the south aisle where a bay of the gallery was removed to accommodate it, and Mr Oldknow himself was in attendance at the official opening ceremony which was reported at some length in the Dorset County Chronicle of 31 May 1883. The organ remained in this position for more than ten years, as a faculty for the addition of the present organ chamber on the north side of the chancel is dated 21 September 1893. The estimated cost was £650 and the architects were Crickmay and Sons of London and Weymouth who designed the chamber to form a symmetrical plan arrangement reflecting St Edward's chapel on the south side. A 14th century window displaced from the north wall of the chancel was re-used in a comparable position in the new work.

The 20th century

A faculty dated 25 July 1903 was for removing the galleries from the aisles, and the rector, hoping apparently to expedite, or perhaps by-pass, the normal faculty process, had written to the bishop personally on 18 July 1903, stating: "My Lord, we are anxious to get this matter settled because the builder who is putting on the new roof is almost ready to take down the scaffolding." This therefore gives the date of the present nave roof, and presumably also of the aisle roofs as they are of similar construction. They are of exposed boarding and rafters divided into four bays by tie beam trusses with wall posts supported by octagonal stone corbels ornamented by an embattled motif. The trusses of the lean-to roofs of the aisles are of half truss form, and all the purlins have arched wind bracing.

West Lulworth
(Holy Trinity)

UNTIL THE 19th century West Lulworth was a chapelry of Winfrith, and the former church, which stood on the north side of the village street almost a quarter of a mile east of the present site, appears to have originated in the 13th century. Sir Stephen Glynne who visited the old church on 20 June 1849 described it as:

"A small church, much altered, comprising nave and chancel, and a low tower on the south side which forms a porch. There has been a modern extension, or enlargement, on the south of the nave with an entirely new wall. The windows on the north of the nave are Third-Pointed, with square heads. The chancel arch, if ever there was any, is removed, and the chancel laid open to the nave. The east window appears to be an original First-Pointed triplet. The tower is very plain Third-Pointed, having square-headed belfry windows, except on the north where is merely a slit. The church has a stone tiled roof. The roof of the nave is leaded, without parapet. The north door has been closed."

The old church was also described by Hutchins' editors (3rd edition: 1861):

"The Chapel of West Lulworth, dedicated to the Holy Trinity, stands near the east end of the vill, and is a small edifice consisting of chancel, nave, south aisle, and tower on the south side of the nave. It contains but little worthy of notice. The tower is a Perpendicular building of two stages with a battlemented parapet slightly advanced, and resting on a moulded string. It apparently incorporates the remains of an Early English tower or porch. A rectangular stair-turret is entered by a narrow pointed doorway with chamfer and stop also apparently Early-English. There are two bells. The aisle is a modern erection... The rector of Winfrith officiated here weekly in Hutchins' time, but of late years there has been a resident curate. The project of erecting this chapelry into a separate benefice is now under consideration."

These two accounts tally well, and together give a relatively clear picture of the old building, even though the architectural terminology used is different. 'First-Pointed' and 'Early-English' are alternative terms for 13th century work, whilst 'Third-Pointed' or 'Perpendicular' generally refer to work of the 15th and early 16th centuries. One relic from the old church, a 16th century flat triangular rear arch, was re-used in the present building to form the inside lintel over the east window of the vestry. It has a carved angel at each end and a widely spaced raised black-letter inscription reading 'Robertus Lulleworth'. There is also a fitting in the chancel in the form of a combined chest and bench seat largely made up of 17th century carved panelling.

The old site was a very restricted one with little opportunity for enlargement, so that the combined effect of accumulated dilapidations and an increasing population led to the inevitable decision to rebuild the church on an entirely new site in a more central position between the old village centre and the later development nearer the cove. In the words of the faculty document, dated 13 May 1869:

" ... the ancient Church of West Lulworth aforesaid together with the Chancel thereof having been ascertained to be in a very dilapidated and dangerous condition and being inadequate to the accommodation of the Inhabitants of the said Parish or Chapelry in their attendance upon Divine Service, ..."

The estimated cost was £1463, and the architect was John Hicks of Dorchester. The drawings are dated 30 August and 18th September 1867, just after Thomas Hardy rejoined Hicks in July 1867 for a second spell as his architectural assistant. Hardy is therefore particularly likely to have been involved in the design and construction of this church, as not only could he have prepared the plans, but he was engaged by Crickmay who took over the practice after Hicks' death on 12 February 1869, specifically to assist in continuing church projects begun by Hicks.

Work must have begun immediately the faculty was granted as the foundation stone of the new church was laid on 1 June 1869 as reported in the Dorset County Chronicle of 3 June:

"On Tuesday ... the foundation stone of the new church in this parish was laid by Lady Selina Bond in the presence of a numerous company of friends and well-wishers of this desirable object... A parchment scroll was sealed up in a bottle and placed in the cavity of the stone, according to custom" ... and on it was recorded the names of the vicar, churchwardens and church building committee.

The church of 1869-70 consists of a nave, chancel, north aisle, north vestry and a tower placed near the south

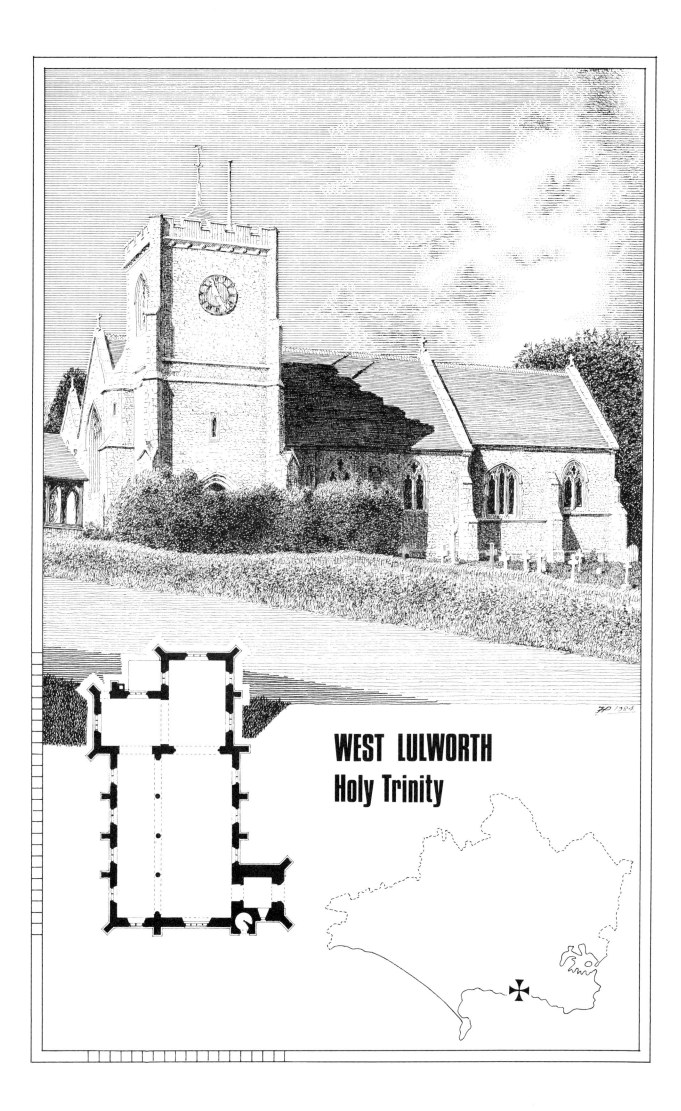

WEST LULWORTH
Holy Trinity

An interesting early 19th century drawing of the old church demolished when the present church was built in 1869-70. The tower was on the south side, and the steps and doorway led to a gallery at the west end of the nave

[Source: West Lulworth church]

west angle where the lower stage serves as an entrance porch. The structural bays are expressed externally by two stage buttresses, diagonally set at the angles, and the windows mostly have trefoil headed lights and varying forms of geometrical and quatrefoil tracery. The tower is in two main stages defined by a double string course, with a stair turret at the north west angle, square at the bottom, octagonal further up, and ending in a pyramidal stone roof at the base of the upper stage. Diagonal buttresses at the angles have gabled offsets in the lower stage and rise as diagonal standards to the top of the parapet which is embattled and ornamented by paterae on the parapet string course. Behind the parapet the tower roof has a tiled pyramidal roof with a weathervane finial rising from its apex.

Internally the arcade is formed of four pointed and keel moulded arches springing from circular columns with square moulded abaci above foliage carved capitals incorporating voluted motifs at the angles. The arches opening from the vestry are similar to those of the arcade, the mouldings of the arch to the north aisle being continuous, whilst those of the arch on the chancel side spring from deep hollow chamfered imposts above chamfered jambs. The chancel arch is of two keel moulded orders springing from chamfered abaci above chamfered responds with central attached shafts having foliage carved capitals. The roof of the chancel takes the form of a six sided polygonal barrel divided into five bays of six boarded panels by moulded ribs, the two eastern bays being separated from the remainder by a larger moulded arched rib springing from wall shafts having foliage carved capitals and corbel brackets. The roofs of the nave and north aisle, both double pitched, are similar and of characteristic Hicks design, having plastered soffites between exposed rafters divided into four bays by arch braced high collar trusses. These are supported by

plain flared stone corbels in the north aisle and by inverted pyramid shaped stone corbels in the nave carved with scalloped ornament and foliage bosses.

The font has a circular bowl ornamented by a band of carved roundels and scalloping to the lower edge supported by a central stem and six perimeter columns, all in marble with foliage carved stone capitals, above a hexagonal base and octagonal step. Similar marble perimeter columns occur on the pulpit which is otherwise of stone ornamented by pointed arcading with prism ornament and supported by a corbelled base having leaf carving in a scale pattern.

The consecration of the new church was reported at some length in the Dorset County Chronicle of 12 May 1870:

"A great and good work has been accomplished in the ancient village of West Lulworth – the erection of the church which was consecrated this (Wednesday) morning. The foundation stone of the sacred structure was laid about twelve months ago by Lady Selina Bond, and the building has progressed in the most satisfactory manner, under the superintendence of Mr G. R. Crickmay, architect, of Weymouth, the original plans having been prepared by the late Mr John Hicks, of Dorchester. The work was begun and carried out according to Mr Crickmay's detailed drawings, Messrs. Wellspring and Son, of Dorchester, being the builders. The old church was, it may be remembered, in a very dilapidated condition, and its thorough and satisfactory restoration was pronounced to be impossible. It was therefore judiciously decided that there should be a new church for the benefit of the parishioners, and to gladden the visitors to this delightful neighbourhood. The work was commenced under the auspices of the Vicar (the Rev. W. Gildea) ...

"The old church stood in the midst of the village, and tourists who frequent the neighbourhood may possibly remember the palpable inadequacy of the building to the wants of the inhabitants around, its dilapidated condition, and the awkward manner in which the cottages on each side intruded upon its precincts, unpleasantly disturbing the impression of sanctity, solemnity, and dignity that we are wont to associate with our ideas of a parish church. The new site is on open ground ... to the west of the present churchyard, and has been chosen with the view of more nearly equalising the distance between the building and the different outlying dwellings of the parish... The whole of the design is carried out excepting the two upper stages of the tower, which are as yet to be left unfinished for lack of the necessary funds. The style the architect has selected is a development of the Early Geometric Gothic, the whole of the detail throughout being treated with that spirit and freedom which the recent close study of this phase of ancient architecture seems to warrant. The carved, moulded, and highly finished portions of the stonework generally are of Bath freestone, the remainder being that of the neighbourhood...

"A more unfavourable day for the opening services could not have been chosen. Heavy rain set in about seven o'clock this morning, and continued throughout the day. The wet and cold kept many friends away, and the attendance of visitors from distant parts was not large. There was nevertheless, a numerous congregation. The church was generally admired. Some of the visitors who arrived early were conducted through the sacred edifice by the vicar and Mr Crickmay (the architect), and it was exceedingly gratifying to learn that numerous and valuable gifts had been received for the completion of the structure. Foremost in the list of the ladies and gentlemen from whom presents have come stands the name of the vicar, who has proved himself a skilful workman. The framework of the reredos, the altar, and the pedestal of the lectern were all executed by himself, and in the task he has displayed considerable skill... The adornment of the three centre panels (of the reredos) was done by Miss Hicks, of Dorchester, daughter of the original architect of the building, the late Mr Hicks. The altar is inlaid with oak from the roof of the old church... The supports of the altar rail are the work of the vicar... The scripture text over one of the chancel arches was done by Mr Benjamin Grassby, of Dorchester. The carving of the columns is also the work of Mr Grassby, who has performed his work in a careful and satisfactory manner. The carving is conventional foliage with natural foliage introduced...

"Luncheon was provided in a tent erected in a field near the church, and there was a numerous party, over whom the Lord Bishop of the diocese presided... We are requested to state that subscriptions are required for the tower, which should be commenced at once for the satisfactory completion of the sacred structure. Communications would be thankfully received by the vicar."

One of West Lulworth's most frequent visitors, the well-known Bishop Wordsworth, bishop of Salisbury 1885-1911, is commemorated by a plaque in the chancel which records that he: "during these years frequently ministered and worshipped here."

Winfrith Newburgh (St. Christopher)

A CHURCH is known to have been in existence here at the time of the domesday survey of 1086 when the hundred of Winfrith covered an area now represented by the present day parishes of Winfrith, East and West Lulworth, Coombe Keynes, and parts of Wool and East Stoke lying south of the river Frome. It is therefore likely that this was a minster church serving an area approximating to the hundred, and although nothing of the original 11th century church now remains visible, several unusual features still apparent in the present building strongly suggest that it was of an axial plan form of nave – tower – chancel as at Studland. Moreover, also as at Studland, it appears to have been remodelled or rebuilt in the 12th century.

In the present plan the unusual proportions of long nave and short chancel are very apparent and alone suggest the existence of a former central tower, particularly as the lower part of a clasping buttress which would have formed its south east angle still remains. In addition the south wall of the nave retains evidence of having been built in two different phases during the 15th century, consistent with such a tower having been taken down when replaced by the present 15th century one at the west end. The unusual thickness of the east wall of the nave is equally suggestive, and the curiously off-centre position of the chancel arch would be accounted for by the nave having been widened to the north when the central tower was removed.

The 12th century
The east wall of the nave consists largely of 12th century work insitu, including the clasping buttress already referred to and the chancel arch which is of two chamfered orders with short corbel shafts having reeded capitals. The arch itself was probably originally semi-

Chancel
arch

circular, but it appears to have been rebuilt to its present pointed form in the 13th century, and although the outer order is continuous with the responds on the chancel side, the outer order of the responds on the nave side continues upwards to the nave roof, but again this unusual arrangement could have resulted from the removal of a former central tower.

WINFRITH NEWBURGH
St Christopher

WINFRITH NEWBURGH probable development

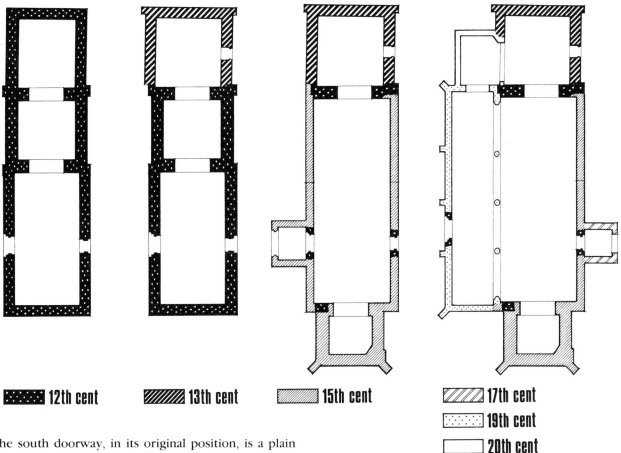

- ▓▓▓ **12th cent**
- ▨▨▨ **13th cent**
- ▨ **15th cent**
- ▨ **17th cent**
- ⬚ **19th cent**
- ☐ **20th cent**

The south doorway, in its original position, is a plain Norman one of two orders, the outer semi-circular and springing from moulded and hollow chamfered abaci above circular jamb shafts with cushion capitals, and the inner with a shallow elliptical head below a plain tympanum. The north doorway, of similar date and originally in the north wall of the nave, was moved to its present position in the north aisle in 1852 when it is said to have been restored, but it would probably be more accurate to describe it as a 19th century replica incorporating some of the original Norman material. Presumably the principal approach to the church has always been from the north, as this doorway is much more elaborate, being of three orders with chevron ornament, two sets of jamb shafts, and an unusual trefoil headed inner archway having a pendant at the apex,

At the west end externally, between the north wall of the tower and its north east buttress, a piece of older work is visible just above ground level which could be the remains of the north west corner of the 12th century nave. If this is so, then it establishes its original length and width and confirms that the nave was subsequently widened to the north to account for the off-centre position of the chancel arch.

South doorway

North doorway

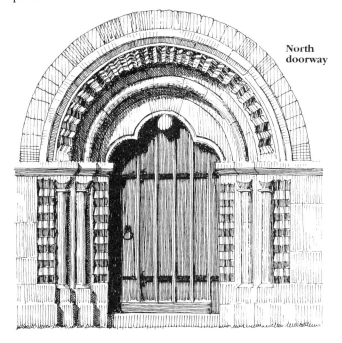

The 13th century

The rebuilding of the upper part of the chancel arch already referred to was probably carried out in association with a general rebuilding of the chancel itself in the 13th century, probably on earlier foundations. The upper part of the east wall has since been rebuilt and the north wall largely disappeared when the organ chamber was added in 1914, but the south wall remains complete from the 13th century to include two lancet windows flanking a priest's doorway with a chamfered segmental pointed head. These windows would originally have been of the usual narrow lancet form, but they have been subsequently widened by the interesting expedient of inserting the trefoiled ogee heads of 14th century windows into the apexes, one of which in the head of the south east window has pierced or sunk spandrels now filled with mortar.

Chancel, south-west window

The 15th century

During the 15th century the nave was rebuilt, probably in association with the addition of the west tower and the consequent removal of the assumed earlier central tower, as suggested by the surviving south wall which retains clear evidence of two phases of rebuilding marked by a change in stone sizes and plinth at a straight joint which extends to about half the height of the wall. West of this point there are two windows of 15th century origin arranged symmetrically on either side of the porch, originally with square heads but now with vertical tracery of 1852. Also in 1852 a complete 15th century window

Nave, south-east window

was moved from the north wall of the nave to its present position in the eastern sector of the south wall. It is a fine example of four cinquefoiled lights with vertical tracery in a segmental pointed head set within a deep outer casement moulding. Two fragments of stained glass depicting red roses on a background of gold leaves still remain in the tracery lights, and three further fragments, of two leopards' heads and part of a priest's head, now reassembled in the south west window of the chancel, may have originally belonged to the same window.

In 1971 when alterations were being carried out in a nearby cottage, an interesting 15th century window head, previously concealed above a low ceiling in a first floor room, was discovered. It is of an unusual form, of four cinquefoil headed lights with vertical tracery featuring a

Window-head, in cottage

central quatrefoil under a shallow segmental pointed head. There can be little doubt that it came originally from the church, possibly from the former east window, as descriptions of the church of 1842 and 1861 include the statements that: "The chancel has the east window deprived of its tracery," and "All the tracery of the east window is destroyed, having been repaired with modern masonry." Mediaeval head stops of a king and bishop on either side of the present east window may have been original label terminations.

The west tower is of three stages with flush square buttresses at the eastern angles, diagonal ones at the western angles, and a spiral staircase unusually contrived largely within the wall thickness at the south west angle necessitating only a shallow projection externally. The parapet is embattled with large grotesque gargoyles on the parapet string course at the angles and third points, making twelve in all. The west window is of three

West window

cinquefoiled lights with open vertical tracery in a pointed head, and the belfry windows are each of two trefoiled lights with a quatrefoil between verticals in a pointed head. Internally the tower arch is pointed and of two

Tower arch

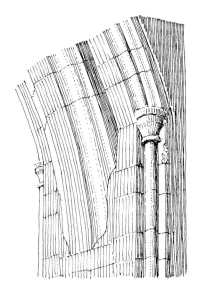

moulded orders, the inner wave moulding dying into the responds and the outer double ogee mouldings springing from angle shafts with moulded capitals. On the south side of the tower externally there is a carved head corbel above a small window in the second stage.

Other mediaeval items include parts of a former gable cross built into the east wall of the south porch, and no less than four scratch dials on the jambs of the priest's door in the south wall of the chancel. A former north porch to the nave, removed when the north aisle was added in 1852, was probably of 15th century date, as there is said to have been a canopied niche over the outer archway. A former wall painting which probably dated from the 15th century rebuilding of the nave is referred to by Hutchins (1st edition: 1774):

"The Church of Winfrith, is situated at the W. end of the parish, and seems to have been dedicated to St Christopher, whose effigy was formerly on the S. wall of the body, but is now plaistered over."

The 17th century

The south porch was added or rebuilt in the 17th century, and has a lightly chamfered semi-circular headed outer archway enclosing a brick and stone tympanum above a segmental headed moulded wooden door frame. Other remains of this period include an oak table with carved rails, a pair of carved chairs with claw feet, and a panel of lead from the tower roof with raised cast letters reading LINARD STROUD THO MEADON 1680 with a ladder represented at the bottom left hand corner.

The 19th century

Sir Stephen Glynne who visited the church in 1842 described the building as it was before the restoration and enlargement of 1852:

"This church derives some interest from its beautiful churchyard, which is shaded by several large trees, and planted with shrubs and flowers; the whole most neatly kept. The walls are much covered with ivy. The building consists of a nave and chancel and west tower. The latter is Rectilinear, good and plain, of three stages and embattled; there is no door. The west window has three lights; that on the second stage is single and square; in the belfry of two lights. The nave is covered with lead; the north and south porches plain, but within the north porch is a beautiful Norman doorway of curious character, verging towards Early English; the outer arch semi-circular, with three tiers of moulding having the roller and double chevron; the shafts have square capitals. The inner door arch is trefoiled, resting on a square abacus on each

side, below which is a rich band of chevron ornament running down to the ground. In the apex of this arch is an ornamented corbel. The north porch has a canopied niche over the outer door. On the south of the nave are two square-headed windows of two lights; on the north is one fine large window of four lights. The arch to the chancel is Early English, rising from shafts, each of which has a Norman capital and abacus, and stands on a bracket of the same character. South of this arch is a square aperture. Some of the windows have a little stained glass. The chancel has the east window deprived of tracery, and on one side of it is a small feathered niche. There are two lancet windows south of the chancel, and one on the north. There is also a square-headed Rectilinear one on the north, and a little stained glass. The font is of cylindrical form, upon a circular base, the upper part of which has mouldings."

In 1852 the church was subject to a major restoration when the nave was to a large extent rebuilt and the north aisle was added. The architect was T. H. Wyatt, the builders were Messrs. Roper and Taylor, and the clerk of works was Moses Lillington. Externally the work is generally in 15th century style conforming to that of the nave and tower, with vertical traceried windows and the structural bays expressed externally by two stage buttresses set diagonally at the angles. Internally, the arcade is somewhat inconsistently in 14th century style, being in four bays of pointed arches of two lightly chamfered orders springing from octagonal piers having moulded capitals and bases. The nave roof is of plastered soffites between exposed rafters divided into four main bays by tie beam trusses having queen posts with arched bracing at the apexes and traceried outer spandrels. The undersides of the tie beams are moulded with central foliage carved bosses, and the bearings have rounded roots merging into short wall posts supported by plain square stone corbels. Each bay is sub-divided by a pair of moulded principal rafters. The double pitched roof of the north aisle is similar to that of the nave, but the trusses are of collar type with traceried apexes, and the stone corbels are moulded. The font is also of 1852 and the sides of its octagonal bowl are ornamented by an angel holding a scroll inscribed 'In memoriam', an IHS monogram, foliage, the symbol of St John Baptist, daffodils, a dove, a rose and a quatrefoil.

Although there appears to have been no faculty, the work of 1852 is well documented in various issues of the Dorset County Chronicle, from which the following extracts are taken:

22 January 1852 – "The Salisbury Diocesan Church Building Association has granted ... £150 towards an additional aisle and other improvements in the parish church of Winfrith Newburgh."

4 March 1852 – Winfrith school had been burnt down, and in connection with this report it was stated that – "The loss of their schoolroom is peculiarly felt by the parish at this time, when they have just taken in hand the restoration and enlargement of their Parish Church."

27 May 1852 – "WINFRITH – Laying the Foundation Stone of a New Aisle to the Parish Church – The parish Church is dedicated to St Christopher, and presents many varied features of ecclesiastical architecture from the very earliest Norman (if not Saxon) to the latest perpendicular. It is proposed to retain as nearly as possible the original features. ... This fine old parish Church, which has long been in a very dilapidated state, is

now (through the exertions of the worthy and esteemed rector, the Rev. George Peloquin Graham Cosserat) undergoing a thorough repair, with the addition of a new aisle, to give increased accommodation to nearly 200 persons, making the total number of sittings 405. On Monday last the ceremony of laying the foundation stone took place at eight o'clock pm., upon which interesting occasion there was assembled a vast concourse of the parishioners, all of whom appeared to feel deeply interested. The worthy Rector, with his family, received the parishioners at the rectory, where tea and other refreshments were provided for all who chose to partake of them. Upon this occasion we were delighted to observe the perfect harmony and affability which prevailed, for here was no distinction of persons, the rich and poor had met together, and they were all made equally welcome by the worthy Rector and his sister. The appointed hour for the ceremony, 8 o'clock, having arrived, the procession formed on the Rectory walks, headed by the Rector... The school children were formed in procession, and, headed by the well-known Winfrith Band proceeded to the Church, where they formed into a circle to witness the ceremony, and the two ladies, Miss Helen Cosserat and Miss A. Foster, took their places near the work. The Rev. Gentleman then offered up two appropriate collects (the people all standing uncovered) ... The foundation stone being raised, Mr Moses Lillington, clerk of the works, handed the trowel and mallet to the ladies, and we were pleased to observe the zeal and animation with which the duty of this novel occupation was discharged by the delicate hands to which it had been assigned. Several coins of the present reign were, according to custom, deposited in the stone. Upon the completion of the ceremony, the choir accompanied by the two flutists, Randall and Baker, commenced chanting the 'Te Deum', the people all joining with reverence and devotion. The Rev. gentleman then in a very appropriate and feeling address ... Their new Church he hoped would present in its arrangements an entire absence of every feature which could in any way indicate a distinction of persons. He intimated that special directions had been given to the architect, T. H. Wyatt, Esq., that all the seats should be of an uniform character and every facility afforded that the congregation might reverently kneel in God's House of Prayer. The blessing having been given, the National Anthem was sung, and the company retired to the lawn adjoining the Rectory, where the band continued playing, and not until night closed the scene did the multitude disperse to their respective homes. Thus ended these most interesting proceedings, which evidently furnished forth a cheerful and hallowed holiday for all. We understand that the contemplated works cannot be completed for less than £1000, towards which, as yet, the Building Committee have only raised £500."

18 November 1852 – Six months later the building fund still stood at only £500, and an appeal was inserted in the Chronicle's advertising columns –
"In making an Appeal to the Public, to those interested in the MAINTENANCE, if not extension of the ministration of the Church of England; the Rector and Churchwardens of Winfrith Newburgh, in the County of Dorset, believe they have a strong case, and one likely to enlist much sympathy.

"The peculiarities of their case may be shortly stated. The sole Proprietor of the Soil in this extensive Parish is a Member of the Roman Catholic Church; this circumstance necessarily calls for constant and anxious watchfulness on the part of the resident Clergy. The population (1600 in all) is so scattered as to require Three Churches, entailing Three separate Parochial administrations, Schools, and Services. Half the Tithes are alienated, and there are no resident Gentry to assist and strengthen the Clergy.

"The church had become, by the neglect of past generations, in a very dilapidated condition: it was quite inadequate for the accommodation urgently demanded by a population of about 800 immediately adjoining it; and altho' EVERY CHILD in this portion of the Parish attends the National School, there was no place in the church for their accommodation. To meet these difficulties, and as far as possible to remove them, the Parish has determined to restore and ENLARGE their Mother Church, so as to afford accommodation for 405 persons. The Farmers (altho' all Tenants at will) have UNANIMOUSLY voted a Parish Rate towards this good work.The Metropolitan and Diocesan Societies have shewn their sanction, by making as large grants as their Rules would permit: still with their assistance and such private donations as have hitherto been received, the promised amount only reaches to £500.

"Plans for the restoration and enlargement of this Church, and the addition of a new Vestry have been prepared by Mr WYATT the Diocesan Architect, at an estimated cost of about £1000. The Rector and Churchwardens earnestly seek assistance to enable them to complete this much needed work.

"P.S. The Church will most probably be re-opened for Divine Service at Christmas.

"SUBSCRIPTIONS will be thankfully received by the REV. G. P. GRAHAM COSSERAT, Winfrith Rectory, Dorchester; MESSRS. J. READER, Winfrith; and R. WHITE, Burton, the Churchwardens; and by MESSRS. ELLIOT and PEARCE, Dorchester Bank, Dorchester." (Then follows a list of subscriptions received up to that time).

27 January 1853 – Presumably the appeal was successful as the church was re-opened on 20 January 1853 – "On Thursday last, the ceremony of re-opening this Church took place, when a Sermon was preached by the Venerable Archdeacon Buckle. The company that arrived in the parish during the morning was very numerous... There were several gentry of the neighbourhood present, besides the architect Mr Wyatt, and the contractors, Messrs. Roper and Taylor. The parishioners in attendance were very numerous and altogether formed a very large congregation. There were two services, morning and evening, the collection amounted to £15. 18s."

The 20th century

The work of 1852 does not appear to have included the present triple lancet east window of the chancel, as Hutchins' editors (3rd edition: 1861) refer only to the older windows from which the original tracery had been removed. It is presumably of later 19th or early 20th century date.

A faculty dated 15 November 1907 was: "to remove the present stove from the Parish Church of Winfrith Newburgh aforesaid," and to replace it by a new heating system of hot water pipes and radiators with a boiler house built against the west wall of the south porch, the whole installation, at an estimated cost of £105, being by Thomas Potter and Sons Ltd., of Fulham. The organ chamber on the north side of the chancel was the subject of a faculty dated 1 December 1913, the estimated cost being £255. 8s., and the architect C. E. Ponting. It is gabled to the north and is lit by a square headed window of two cinquefoiled lights: internally it opens to the north aisle by a pointed arch of two chamfered orders, and to the chancel by an opening spanned by an oak lintel with moulded arrises.

The chancel roof was renewed or repaired during this century as the tie beam is said to have been hewn from a locally grown tree within living memory. The roof itself is of exposed oak boarding and rafters divided into two bays by a truss which has large raking struts and a massive cambered tie beam.

Wool
(Holy Rood)

UNTIL THE 19th century Wool was a chapelry of Coombe Keynes, and although the inhabitants gained some measure of independence in 1384 by obtaining the right to perform burials in their own churchyard, the church nevertheless remained a chapel in status until 1844 when Wool became a separate parish. A considerable rebuilding and enlargement in 1865-66 resulted in the destruction of a great part of the old church, but much is known of it from plans and elevations of the former building and pre 1865 descriptions.

Hutchins (1st edition: 1774) says:

"The Chapel of Wool is a chapel of ease to Comb-Keynes, and officiated in once a fortnight by the vicar, for which he has a salary of £5 per annum, paid by Edward Weld, Esq., in lieu of all glebe and tithes. It is situated in the S. part of the vill, and consists of a chancel, body, narrow N. isle, and a low embattled tower, in which are four bells. At the upper end of the N. isle is a chapel divided from the other part by an arch, and belonging to Bindon. West of this chapel was the burial place of the Turbervilles of Woolbridge. On the wall, 'M. T. Matthew Turbervill'. There is nothing remarkable in it, but an ancient pulpit-cloth, well preserved, said to have belonged to Bindon-abbey. It is of brown velvet, and on it are embroidered in gold, the twelve apostles; but it is most probable it belonged to Bindon Chapel, and was preserved when that and the house were burnt in the civil wars. The inhabitants of this chapelry maintain their own chapel and poor, and bury in the chapel yard."

Sir Stephen Glynne visited the church on 19 June 1849 and described it as:

"A small church, consisting of nave and chancel, each with north aisle, and north and south porch, and a western tower. The whole built of stone. There are some First-Pointed portions; of which character is the arcade of the nave, having three arches with circular columns of which the capitals are moulded. The western respond has good foliage. There is a curious triple chancel arch, with light octagonal piers having no capitals. The eastern pier beyond the arcade is very large and contains a square opening now glazed. The windows of the nave are Third-Pointed, chiefly square-headed. The chancel has First-Pointed lancets and a Priest's door on the south. The east window Third-Pointed. On the north of the chancel is a plain continuous arch opening to the aisle or chapel, with a large wall space eastward. There is a similar arch between the aisle of the nave and that of the chancel. On the north side of the tower arch is a staircase with openings facing eastward. There is a hideous north gallery. The tower arch has fair mouldings. The tower is Third-Pointed, with battlement and buttresses set away from the angles; at the south-east, a polygonal turret terminated by a pyramidal finishing. The belfry window of two lights, a slit in the second stage, and no west door. Instead of the eastern belfry window is an open quatrefoil. The porches are also Third-Pointed, – the outer doors having shafts, and the north porch quatrefoil openings on the sides. The font is Third-Pointed, the bowl octagonal, panneled with quatrefoils. There are no parapets. The nave is slated, the aisle leaded, the chancel tiled. In the churchyard are seen the odd names of Cram and Phone."

In the foregoing description the terms 'First-Pointed' and 'Third-Pointed' mean 13th and 15th century respectively.

The 13th century

From the above descriptions and others taken in conjunction with the faculty plans of the old building, it is clear that the original 13th century church consisted of a nave, chancel and narrow north aisle, most of which has disappeared in the course of rebuildings in the 15th and 19th centuries. The original north arcade does, however, remain in its original position to form the centre two bays of the present north arcade, the pointed arches being entirely of brown heathstone and of two chamfered orders springing from a central circular column with a moulded capital and base having spur ornaments, with matching half column responds which also still remain to form parts of larger columns. Evidently the original 13th

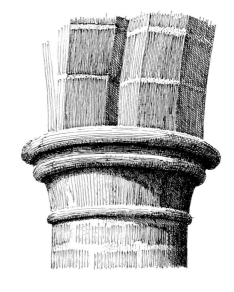

North arcade capital

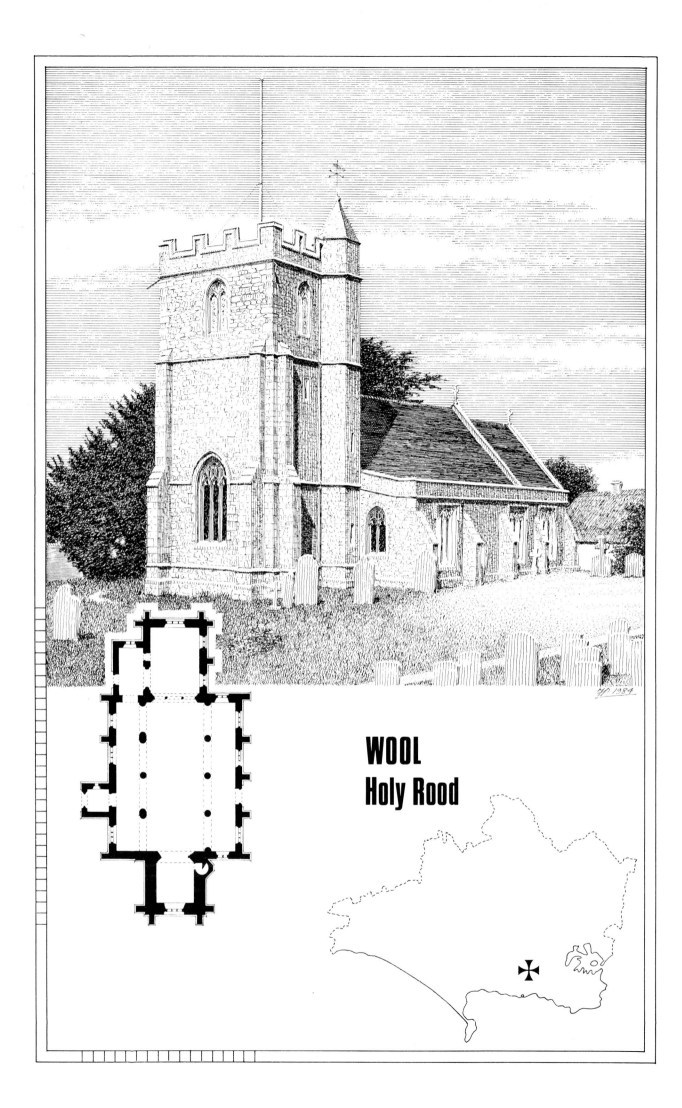

WOOL
Holy Rood

WOOL development

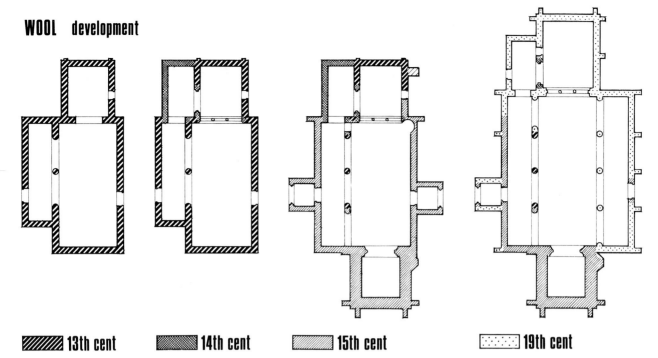

13th cent   14th cent   15th cent   19th cent

century chancel survived in essence until 1865, as Sir Stephen Glynne refers to lancet windows which still remained in 1849.

The 14th century

A chapel was evidently added to the north side of the chancel during this period, as 14th century archways which led into it from the north aisle and chancel were re-used in comparable positions in the north east vestry of 1865-66. They are both of two chamfered orders, the arch to the chancel being pointed above similarly moulded responds, whilst the narrower arch to the north aisle is triangular and springs from square responds of 1865-66. The unusual triple chancel arch is of similar date and was also re-used in 1865-66 some nine feet east of its former position. The arches are pointed and of two chamfered orders, the inner order being continuous with the intermediate octagonal columns, and the arcade is now framed by an overall pointed arch of 1865-66 which encloses a plain tympanur above it.

The 15th century

During this period the nave and north aisle were rebuilt, north and south porches were added or rebuilt, and the west tower was added. The north aisle was

15th century window

presumably rebuilt on the original foundations as the earlier narrow form was retained, but it was lengthened to the west as indicated by the west arch of the arcade, which although of 15th century date, repeats the earlier details of the 13th century arches except at the west respond where the arch springs from a foliage carved corbel. The north wall of the aisle still largely survives from the 15th century and contains the triangular headed north doorway with unusual rounded and hollow chamfer mouldings, flanked by two windows each of three cinquefoiled lights in a square head. The triangular rear arch of the easternmost of these two windows is of interest in that one side is formed by a slab of stone intended for some panelled feature with cinquefoil cusping marked out but uncarved. Two similar windows and a doorway were re-used in the 1865-66 south aisle from comparable positions in the south wall of the nave.

Similar two light windows from the east and north walls of the north chapel were also re-used in 1865-66, one in the east wall of the vestry and one in the north wall of the north aisle at the east end. The 15th century north porch,

15th century window and quatrefoil

although rebuilt in 1865-66, retains the original pointed entrance arch which is wave and ogee moulded with jamb shafts, and a small quatrefoil opening in the east wall. A similar 15th century south porch was not reinstated.

The west tower is of three stages with an embattled parapet, square inset buttresses and a hexagonal stair turret at the south east angle ending in a distinctive pyramidal stone roof above parapet level. In the upper stage there is a small quatrefoil opening in the east wall and belfry windows in the remainder, each of two cinquefoiled lights filled with pierced stone panels of 1865-66, below blank tracery in the form of a quatrefoil between verticals within a pointed head. The west window is of three trefoiled lights with vertical tracery in

The font

West window

The 15th century font is semi-octagonal and built against a column, the sides of the bowl being ornamented by sunken quatrefoiled roundels. A second font of 13th century date at the east end of the south aisle is from Coombe Keynes church. An interesting mediaeval cresset stone, a form of oil lamp with four holes for wicks, is preserved in the church, and was discovered in the course of the work of 1865-66 built into the wall between the chancel and north chapel.

a pointed head, and the pointed tower arch has continuous wave, hollow chamfer and ogee mouldings, the inner ogee being represented on the jambs by attached shafts having foliage carved capitals.

Cresset stone

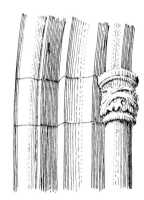

Tower arch

The 'pulpit-cloth' referred to by Hutchins was actually an altar frontal made up from portions of late 15th and early 16th century vestments in eight vertical strips, four of which feature embroidered standing figures in canopied niches probably representing saints or biblical characters. The vestments are likely to have come from Bindon abbey after the Reformation and to have been made into a frontal at some later date. Owing to its fragile and vulnerable nature it was placed on loan at the Dorset County Museum in 1886.

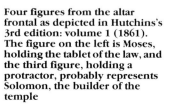

Four figures from the altar frontal as depicted in Hutchins's 3rd edition: volume 1 (1861). The figure on the left is Moses, holding the tablet of the law, and the third figure, holding a protractor, probably represents Solomon, the builder of the temple

Interior, showing the
13th century north
arcade on the left, and
the unusual 14th
century triple arcade to
the chancel
[Photograph:
Colin Graham]

The 18th century

A royal arms of George III (1760-1820) dating from the earlier years of his reign, before 1800, is painted on a wooden panel additionally inscribed 'J. Brown. Churchwarden', and hangs on the west wall of the north aisle.

Before 1865 there were galleries in the north aisle and across the west end of the nave. They were probably of 18th or early 19th century date, and were approached not only by internal staircases, but by an outside flight of steps against the east wall of the north porch leading to an upper doorway in the north wall of the aisle. The former box pews were probably of similar date, and Hutchins' editors (3rd edition: 1861) refer to some aspects of the old seating arrangements:

"Nearly one-third of the seats are free; the remainder, by old-established custom, are considered to belong to different houses in the village, and held by successive occupiers of the same. One large seat is reckoned to belong, by prescription, to Woolbridge House, which is beyond the bounds of the parish, and has been so held since the time of the Turbervilles. An aged parishioner, upwards of ninety in 1858, stated that she had heard that the Turbervilles had first obtained their right to the seat by providing, on some occasion, oak timber for the repairs of the church."

The 19th century

Evidently some extensive repair works were undertaken during the summer of 1838 when an old parish register, normally kept in an iron chest in the chancel, was temporarily transferred to the home of one of the churchwardens for safekeeping. This ironically resulted in the register being lost for more than 50 years until returned to the parish by way of a London firm of solicitors in 1889.

Hutchins' editors (3rd edition: 1861) refer to changes in the village during the early 19th century and to alterations in the church in 1852:

"The church is conveniently situated, on gently rising ground, in the southern part of the village. There is a tradition among the people, that some time ago it formed the central point in the village; and within the memory of the present generation, changes have taken place which have made it less so than formerly, some houses near the church having been pulled down, and others built at a greater distance, in the common, Bindon lane, &c...

"In 1852, the interior arrangement of the church was improved by the removal of the singing-gallery to its present position, behind the tower arch. It formerly extended much further into the church, and was a great source of disfigurement."

A flute still preserved in the church would have been played regularly in the gallery referred to.

An appeal appeared in the advertising columns of the Dorset County Chronicle of 28 July 1864:

"An urgent appeal is made in behalf of this CHURCH by the Parishioners of Wool ... The Architect, Mr HICKS, of Dorchester, has stated that he considers that holding of Divine Service in the Church in its present state is highly dangerous, as the roof is fast giving way. It is proposed to rebuild the Nave with the exception of the North Wall, and to add a new Aisle, by which about 60 additional sittings will be gained. The cost of the work in the plainest way, keeping it in unison with the present building, has been estimated to be £1,000. Subscriptions will be thankfully received."

This was followed soon afterwards by a faculty dated 23 December 1864 which stated that it was intended "wholly to take down the same Church and Chancel (with the exception of the Tower and portions of the North and West Walls of the Nave, Porch and Arcade) and in lieu thereof to erect fit and complete upon the same site and adjacent portions of the churchyard a substantial and durable church and chancel upon a larger scale with the additions of a South Aisle and Vestry Room and extending the Chancel Twelve feet ten inches into the Churchyard." The estimated cost was at that time stated to be £1,160, and the architect was John Hicks of Dorchester.

The work was carried out generally in accordance with the wording of the faculty, the nave, north aisle and arcade being extended by one bay to the east and the chancel rebuilt on a slightly larger scale eastward of its former position. The entirely new south aisle was built in

An interesting pencil drawing from the north east before the rebuilding and restoration of 1865-66. The name R. H. BOES which appears on the side of the table tomb in the centre foreground may be that of the artist

[Source: Dorset County Museum collection]

imitation of the north aisle re-using the old south door and two windows, and all the new work is in 15th century style with square headed and vertical traceried windows. This style was not however applied internally where the eastward extension of the north arcade and the whole of the south arcade are copied from the pair of 13th century arches which still remain, although the new work is in Corsham stone with only small amounts of brown heathstone introduced at random.

All the roofs were renewed, those of the nave and chancel being of typical Hicks design with plastered soffites between exposed rafters. The chancel roof is divided into two bays by three arch braced principals with hammer beam feet supported by stone angel bust corbels, whilst that of the nave is divided into four bays by five crossed arch braced principals supported by folige carved stone corbels. The aisle roofs, of shallow lean-to form, are of diagonal boarding in alternating directions laid on exposed joists and divided into four bays by raking principals with arch braced feet against the outside walls supported by carved stone head corbels.

The re-opening of the church was reported in the Dorset County Chronicle of 30 August 1866:

" ... the re-opening of Wool Church, after having been restored, beautified, and improved in a manner that must rejoice the heart of every parishioner... In the place of a dilapidated, ruinous, circumscribed edifice, with all sorts of futile contrivances to make it tenantable and weathertight, there is now a comfortable and commodious church, suited to all the requirements of the parishioners, besides being a worthy monument of the liberality of the surrounding inhabitants. The work has been one of no small difficulty, owing to peculiar circumstances in reference to the principal landholding interest of the parish... To Mr Hicks, architect, of Dorchester, was confided the task of preparing the plans of the new edifice, and all who have seen it agree that he has discharged his duty in a manner at once efficiently and worthy of his professional reputation. The execution of the work was entrusted to Mr Wellspring, builder, of Dorchester, who, it is acknowledged, has skilfully and thoroughly carried out the ideas of the architect... The original roof was waggon shaped; but by lapse of time had

become excessively dilapidated, so that at last, rather less than two years since, it was found absolutely necessary to close the church, and since then the services have been conducted in the school-room until the re-opening. The old roof was covered with stone tiles, but some years since these were removed from one side, and slates substituted, thus destroying the equilibrium of pressure on the walls, and contributing in great measure to the evil that was sought to be averted. There existed also a gallery on the north side, and at the west end. The pews were high and cumbrous, of the description that generally prevailed in country churches until late years... The roof is open-timbered, of tolerably high pitch, the circular ribs resting upon stone corbels, those in the nave carved in natural foliage of oak, maple, vine, &c., by Mr Grassby, of Dorchester; the aisle corbels have carved heads of the 15th century style... In the former church a very fine stone font was built into the extreme pier at the north side at the west end; but this has been removed and attached to the same pier, but on the east side of it. Over the chancel screen ... the architect has caused to be erected a relieving arch, which is filled in with a tympanum... The roof timbers of the chancel are supported on Bath stone corbels carved with angels... We may here mention that the carved stone corbels are the work of Mr Bolton, of Worcester, and Mr Grassby, of Dorchester, both of whom deserve great praise... The pulpit constitutes a very handsome portion of the church accessories. It is half octagonal in shape, and is formed of Corsham stone, and executed by Mr Grassby. It has a moulded and battlemented cornice, beneath which is a running sprig of passion flower. The centre panel contains the vesica piscis and cross with the monogram I.H.S., with crown above, the whole ornament being formed of alabaster. The spandrels are carved in natural foliage, the angles of the principal front with running sprigs of lilies. In the panels to the right and left are quatrefoils, with the Alpha and Omega in alabaster. We may note among further details that the dressings of the exterior new work are of Box stone and the interior of Corsham stone... In the tower the belfry windows have been filled with perforated stone instead of the bricks that occupied the openings under the old order of things. A ringing floor has also been erected to replace the gallery on which the ringers formerly stood to exercise their office. The bells have been furnished with new carriages. A new organ is also to be observed; it is placed in the chancel aisle, and was supplied by Walker, of London. It is of fair power and tone considering its size, and has five stops: Open and stop diapasons, principal, fifteenth and dulciana."

The report goes on to describe the re-opening service itself and the customary luncheon party for the invited guests: "This took place in a tent erected in a field belonging to Mrs Hyde, of Spring Field Cottage. The repast was provided by Mr May, of the Black Bear Inn."

The 20th century

In 1907 a sixth bell was added to the peal, and all the bells were rehung in a new steel and iron frame by Messrs. Gillett and Johnston of Croydon. More recent work has included the formation of a small chapel at the east end of the north aisle in 1970 when the archway between the vestry and chancel was filled by a modern pierced stone screen.

Worth Matravers
(St. Nicholas)

THIS IS the second most complete Norman church in the Purbeck area, dating from early in the 12th century and contemporary with the nave at Studland, having very similar corbel tabling which still remains under the eaves of both the nave and chancel. As it stands today the church is probably very similar to its original early 12th century general form and appearance, and although it appears to have been altered and extended later in the 12th century and partially rebuilt during the 13th and 14th centuries, more recent works in the 18th and 19th centuries have effectively obscured any clear evidence of these subsequent developments.

The 12th century

The original early 12th century church consisted of a nave, chancel and west tower, all of which still survive in essence apart from the east and south walls of the chancel and the eastern part of the south wall of the nave which have been subsequently rebuilt. Original features include the shallow pilaster buttresses at the four corners of the nave, and three round headed windows at high level in

Norman
corbel table
and window

the north and south walls of the nave, the south east window being a replica of 1869. The corbel tables under the eaves of the nave and chancel are also original, although some sections, notably on the south side of the chancel and south eastern part of the nave, must have been retained and re-used when these sections were later rebuilt. The corbels are very similar to those at Studland and are carved with devices and figures which include various human and animal heads, some in grotesque form, a squatting man, a rabbit, a bird and bird's head. A further grotesque corbel now inside the chancel above the priest's door may also have come from the corbel tabling.

North
doorway

The north doorway is also original, although its segmental or three sided head has since been replaced by a plain flat one, and on either side of it pilaster buttresses arch over parabolically to support a pilaster buttress centrally above it. The south door was originally similar, and although the upper pilaster buttress still remains, those at the sides were removed to accommodate the later 12th century doorway.

The west tower is in three diminishing stages defined by small chamfered offsets and originally with plain quoins, the clasping buttresses at the outer angles having been added in 1869. The belfry windows are small and square headed, of two lights on the north side and of one light on the remainder, the head of that on the east side being chamfered off to a segmental shape on the outside face. At the top there is a plain corbel table which originally probably formed the eaves of a pyramidal roof much as at present. The present roof is entirely of 1869 and replaced a former plain parapet. The tower arch is of one plain order springing from chamfered imposts above plain square responds, and the original round arch has since been rebuilt to its present pointed form.

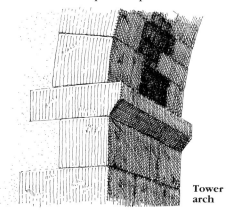

Tower
arch

WORTH MATRAVERS
St Nicholas

The chancel arch and south doorway are of mid 12th century date, and together with chevron ornamented parts of another door or archway of similar date re-used inside the south porch archway, must have been introduced later into the original building. The chancel arch is a large and very fine one, semi-circular and stilted, of three orders on the west side and of two on the east, all with characteristic chevron ornament and jamb shafts having scalloped capitals. Flanking it on the nave side are the carved jambs of former low level side altar recesses, seemingly incompatible with the width of the nave, giving rise to the RCHM'S suggestion that the whole archway might have been brought from elsewhere, perhaps after the Reformation. The stilted form of the arch could also have resulted from such an adaptation to fit a narrower building.

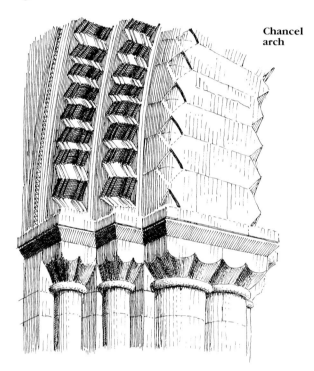

Chancel arch

On the other hand the archway may have been built in the mid 12th century with the view of ultimately widening the nave or of adding transepts, particularly as a former south chapel, demolished in the 18th century, which took a transeptal form at the the east end of the nave appears to have been added at about the same time. It is said to have been demolished in 1774 when its materials were re-used to build the present south porch, so that the mid 12th century chevron ornamented archway re-used inside the porch arch presumably came from it. In addition, Hutchins' description of the church (1st edition: 1774) before the demolition of the south chapel, also suggests that it was of 12th century date:

"The church is situate on the side of a hill, N. of the parish and consists of a body, chancel, and a small S. isle. The tower is plain, containing three bells. The whole fabric is tiled, and is dark and ancient. It is dedicated to St Nicholas. On the S. is an oval arch, which seems to have been an entrance into another isle now demolished. Near the top of the tower, and all round the body, chancel and isle, near the eaves, is a fascia projecting about six inches, most of the stones of which are carved into human heads. On the S. side is a place for holy water; in the E. wall two niches."

All that remains of the south chapel is a squint, now glazed on the outside, and a blocked triangular headed doorway in the south wall of the nave, both of indeterminate date. Hutchins' reference to a stoup on the south side suggests that it also served as a porch, and the "oval arch" on the south side of the nave must refer to the

Blocked doorway in south wall

The interior, showing the round-headed rear arches of the windows and doorways, and the magnificent Norman chancel arch

[Photograph: Colin Graham]

parabolic pilasters of the original south doorway, indicating that it had been blocked in favour of an entrance by way of the south chapel or transept. It can be inferred therefore that the present south doorway also formed part of the former south chapel and that it was moved to its present position in 1774 in conjunction with building the south porch. Its semi-circular head and jambs have chevron ornament enclosing a tympanum above the doorway with a much mutilated carving considered to represent the Coronation of the Virgin, the damage to it being traditionally attributed to bullets fired by Parliamentary forces from Poole in 1645.

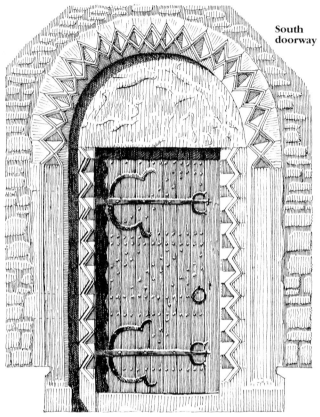

South doorway

The 13th century

During this period the south wall of the chancel was rebuilt with a large battered plinth, and incorporating two lancet windows flanking a narrow pointed priests' doorway, the original corbel tabling being re-used at eaves level. At the same time two similar lancets were inserted in the north wall of the chancel, and a narrower lancet was inserted in the north wall of the nave at the east

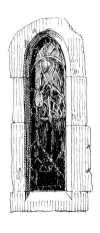
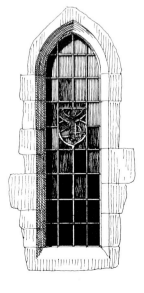

Nave lancet and chancel lancet windows

end. A similar lancet in an opposing position on the south side of the nave is of 1869.

Four coffin lids in the chancel and south porch are of late 13th or early 14th century date, and part of another in the porch was ploughed up in April 1957 in a field about a mile from St Aldhelm's chapel where it covered a burial.

Chancel, east window

The 14th century

During the first half of the 14th century the east wall of the chancel was rebuilt in ashlar work to include a window of three trefoiled ogee headed lights with reticulated tracery in a pointed head. A trefoil headed piscina recess with a plain round bowl in the east wall of the chancel and a cinquefoil headed niche above it, now containing a modern figure of St Nicholas, both appear to have formerly been in the south chapel according to Hutchins' account, and another piscina or stoup bowl now forming part of a credence table is said to have been discovered in the churchyard. Part of the canopy of a

Niche with modern St Nicholas, above a piscina

**An etching by A. Tracey
showing the church
from the south-east**

[Source: Dorset County
Museum collection]

former niche, reset on the east wall of the porch, was found in a neighbouring farmhouse and placed in the church during the incumbency of the Rev. A. Kemp (vicar 1843-50). No doubt it came originally from the church.

The 15th and 16th centuries

There is remarkably little later mediaeval work in the church, there being only a scratch dial in the south wall of the porch, presumably from the former south chapel, and a large 15th century coffin lid in the churchyard. A former 16th century window in the north wall of the nave referred to by Hutchins' editors (3rd edition: 1861): "a square Elizabethan one, to give light to the pulpit," was removed and the opening carefully walled up in 1869.

The 18th century

As referred to before, the former south chapel or transept was demolished and its materials re-used to form the present south porch, and although one of the stones on the south jamb of the entrance arch has scratched initials and date IT 1741, the work is said to have been carried out in 1774. This latter date seems the more likely as the chapel was still standing according to the account by Hutchins who died in 1773.

No account of this church would be complete without reference to the grave of Benjamin Jesty in the north part of the churchyard, and the self explanatory epitaph on the headstone is often quoted:

"(Sacred) To the memory of Benjm. Jesty (of Downshay) who departed this Life April 16th 1816 aged 79 years. He was born at Yetminster in this County, and was an upright honest Man: particularly noted for having been the first Person (known) that introduced the Cow Pox by Inoculation, and who from his great strength of mind made the Experiment from the Cow on his Wife and two Sons in the year 1774."

The 19th century

The font, in 15th century style, is of early 19th century date, with an octagonal bowl decorated by a group of four quatrefoils in diaper pattern on each face on an octagonal stem having trefoil headed panels. The west gallery is also of early 19th century date, and before 1869 was lit by a dormer window on the south side of the nave.

In 1864 moves were afoot to restore and enlarge the church as reported in the Dorset County Chronicle of 28 July 1864:

"We are glad to note another step in the way of church restoration in our diocese. A vestry meeting lately held in this parish passed an unanimous resolution that the vicar and churchwardens be appointed a committee, with power to add to their number, for the purpose of restoring their ancient church ... It is proposed to rebuild the ancient chantry, and thereby to add forty seats to the church, which are very much needed in the accommodation. The estimate, as given by Mr Hicks, of Dorchester, will not exceed £800."

However, plans to rebuild the south chapel did not materialise, but the restoration was the subject of a faculty dated 26 June 1868. It was proposed: " ... to take down and rebuild the unsound portions of the walls of the said Building and to entirely repair and restore the Tower; to restore and reglaze the windows; to re-roof the building; to remove the whole of the floors, paving, pews, seats and internal fittings of the said Church and Chancel and entirely refloor, repave, reseat and refit the same."

The estimated cast was £1,000. The plans and specification are undated and carry no architect's name, so that it is uncertain whether or not John Hicks (who died in February 1869) continued to have any concern in the work. The specification is remarkably brief, and the requirement to bond in with and match older work seems to have been so successfully observed that it is now difficult to distinguish the work then carried out. The specification is consequently of interest:

"To take down such portions of the old walls as are unsound, more especially the upper portions of the S. wall, and rebuild with the old stone as far as it will go making up the deficiency with new of a similar kind. Great care to be taken to follow the bonding of the old work.

"Fill in the spaces in the old walls where stonework may have fallen out and rebed all loose stones and generally repair and make good walling.

"Remove the modern windows and substitute new stone ditto to correspond with those of the earlier date and make good stonework around same.

"The Tower to be strengthened by wrought iron ties and generally repaired where unsound.

"Repair and restore to their original form the defaced pier caps and arches of Chancel arch.

"Frame and fix new open timber roof of the ancient type carefully re-using such of the old timbers ribs and arches of the existing roof as are in good condition, and stain an oak colour.

"Reseat the whole of the church and put new wood floors and joists under seating, make provision for ventilating same.

"Repave the pathways of Church, clean and replaster the inside face of walls."

Before 1869 the capitals of the chancel arch on the north side had been cut away to accommodate a sounding board above the pulpit. The roofs of the nave and chancel are similar, of plastered soffites between exposed rafters divided into bays by trusses, two in the chancel and five in the nave, having massive square tie beams supporting king posts and arched struts.

The 20th century

A faculty dated 7 October 1904 was for an oak reredos which was apparently not proceeded with, and a faculty dated 7 December 1905 was for "a temporary Chancel Screen (to be ultimately removed to the Tower Arch of the said Church) ... and to be replaced on such removal by a permanent Screen of iron or other material." This screen is now under the tower arch, and the proposal to erect a more elaborate one under the chancel arch was fortunately not carried out.

The organ, although modern, is of some interest in that it was built in 1922 specifically for organ examinations in a music school. It was designed by Noel Bonavia-Hunt and built by Messrs. Foskett with three manuals and several experimental stops. It was renovated and rebuilt in Worth church where it was dedicated on 5 February 1958.

Worth Matravers
(St. Aldhelm's Chapel)

THIS LITTLE Norman building, dramatically situated on the windswept headland of St Aldhelm's Head, is not a parochial chapel and never has been, but it is of particular interest, and it seems appropriate to include it among the parish churches of Purbeck. It was built during the second half of the 12th century and has been little altered since, so that with its unchanging backdrop of sky, sea and grass, the chapel and its surroundings must together look very much as they did when the Norman builders completed their work some 800 years ago.

The unique position of the chapel has inevitably given rise to various legends concerning its origin, one being that it was founded by St Aldhelm himself, but he died in 709, more than 400 years before the chapel was built; although it is possible that he might have founded an earlier chapel on the same site. Another legend says it was a memorial to a young bride, built by her father, who, standing on the headland had watched helplessly as the ship in which she and her husband were sailing was wrecked on the rocky shore below; the intention being that the chapel would also serve as a guide and warning to other ships. At least its prime function seems to have been to warn shipping of the dangers of this rocky headland, as the chapel had no parochial status, and its priest was paid by the Crown as related by Hutchins' editors (3rd edition: 1861):

" ... it was anciently served by a royal chaplain. It had no endowment, and no institutions to it are found in the Sarum registers. It does not appear to have been in ecclesiastical connection with the parish of Worth, nor with any religious establishment. In the time of King Henry III (1216-1272) the chapel of St Aldhelm in Purbeck, and the chapel of St Mary in Corfe Castle, were served by two chaplains, who were paid by the Crown through the hands of the sheriff of the county. Their united salary was then 100s. a-year, 50s. a-year being the common stipend of a royal chaplain... in the valor of 1291 ... the chapel of St Aldhelm is rated at 20s. and on the assessment of the aid of the 6th Hen. VI (1427) 'the parish of the chapel of St Aldem' is spoken of. It was still taxed at 20s. but there were no inhabitants."

The building itself is of considerable interest, being square on plan, with an impressive interior divided structurally into four quadripartite vaulted compartments springing from a central column, more like a Norman undercroft chapel beneath a large building than a small isolated above-ground chapel. Pilaster-like vaulting shafts with chamfered abaci, and the similarly shaped vaulting ribs form intersections at the crowns of the vaults by cross shaped keystones, each with an incised diagonal cross.

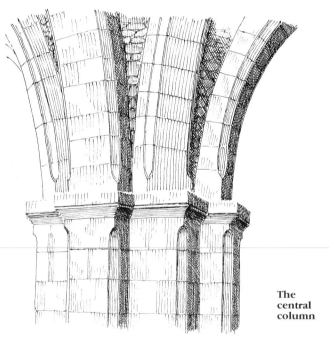

The central column

The vaulting supports a solid stone pyramidal roof faced with Purbeck stone slates, with a raised central drum now supporting a cross of 1873, but originally no doubt carried up as some heavier superstructure as suggested by the presence of the central column beneath. There have been various conjectures as to the nature of this original superstructure: possibly housing for a large bell the tolling of which, although useful in fog, would have been less effective in tempestuous weather, or perhaps some tall feature intended mainly as a navigation aid. 19th century opinion favoured the view that it had supported a fire cresset for a beacon to act as an early form of lighthouse, accounting for the solid stone roof and the complete absence of any timber in the structure.

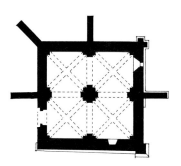

WORTH MATRAVERS
St Aldhelm's Chapel

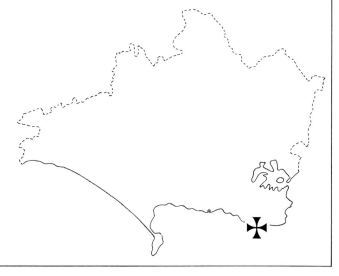

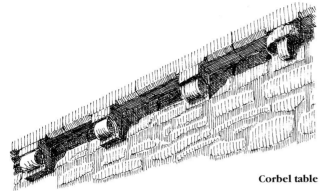

Corbel table

Apart from the four much later and rather prominent raking buttresses, the exterior walls are largely original, with the remains of a battered plinth on the south east and south west sides, an original clasping buttress at the south angle, a slightly later, perhaps 13th century pair of buttresses at the east angle, and under the eaves on the north east side, an original corbel table with shaped corbels all of differing designs, mostly plain, except one which is carved with a spiral motif. The chapel is lit only by one small round headed window, originally unglazed, but with external rebates for a shutter. In the south west

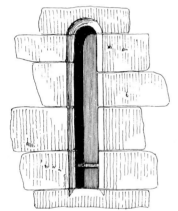

The single Norman window

wall internally there is a plain recess with a sloping base as if it might have been another window originally, and the single doorway is semi-circular headed of two stop

chamfered orders with chamfered imposts and a moulded external label having nailhead enrichment. Around the chapel there are the remains of an earthwork embankment perhaps indicating that in former times the area immediately surrounding the chapel was enclosed by a palisade to give some measure of protection from the severe winds in such an exposed position.

No doubt the chapel ceased to be used as such after the Reformation, and by the end of the 18th century it had become in a dilapidated condition as recorded by Hutchins' editors (2nd edition: 1796):

"Holes have been made in the roof, and South side, and it is likely to be soon in ruins, from want of care to preserve and repair so curious a piece of antiquity."

Soon after this the chapel was repaired at the expense of the landowner, William Morton Pitt, presumably before 1807 when his estates were sold to John Scott (later to become the first Earl of Eldon), and the prominent raking buttresses probably date from this restoration. They are referred to by Hutchins' editors (3rd edition: 1861) as "modern buttresses of hideous form," and although they are somewhat obtrusive they have undoubtedly played a vital role in preserving the building from total collapse, and have now become a familiar and accepted part of the building. A further and more complete restoration is said to have been carried out in 1873 or 1874 at the expense of the Earl of Eldon.

During the latter part of the 19th century the chapel had been used at various times as a stable and as a storeroom for the coastguards, and later as a coastguards' chapel, presumably after the 1873/4 restoration. In earlier times, particularly during the 17th and 18th centuries when its former use as a chapel had been long forgotten, the deserted and isolated building came to be regarded as a place of mystery and superstition, and became known as 'The Devil's Chapel'. The central pillar in particular was believed to possess special powers, when by inserting a pin in a hole at the top it was believed that any wish would be granted, the potency of the spell being no doubt reinforced by scratching the wisher's initials on the column, to account for the number of initials and 17th and 18th century dates still to be found on it. This practice persisted well into this century as pins, including hair-pins, were reported as being seen in the hole on DNHAS visits to the chapel in 1893, 1922 and 1930. H. J. Moule, reading a paper to the Society at the chapel in 1893 (DNHAS Proceedings, Vol. 14, p 75-79) stated:

"For this, like St Katherine's, Abbotsbury, was a wishing chapel. The votary dropped a pin into a hole in the central pier and wished. It has often been done within the last ten years, the Vicar of Worth tells me. Nay, there was a pin in the hole at the time of reading this paper. Moreover, on Whit-Thursday, Worth fair-day and club-day, the people went with music to St Aldhelm's, decked the grey sombre interior with flowers, and danced there, as the Siestas do before Seville high altar. It is a strange thought that this Chantry for sailor's masses should come to be called the Devil's Chapel — to be a dancing place — and, as in my remembrance, a house for coastguard stores."

The Norman doorway